Willing to Walk on Water is a practical and profound invitation to all who hesitate on the shores of the miraculous. Not only is this book engaging, it's empowering. You will be encouraged by stories from Caroline's life and the lives of so many others who consistently make a difference to the beloved broken. Read and believe that your life will open up and touch thousands.

LISA BEVERE
Author and speaker; cofounder of Messenger International

In the face of staggering statistics of hurt and pain in the world, Caroline Barnett helps us see that we are part of God's answers to the world's problems. Be inspired. Step out in the direction of God's calling in your life. Be *willing to walk on water.*

STEVEN FURTICK
Lead pastor of Elevation Church; author of the *New York Times* bestseller *Greater*

willing to walk on water

STEP OUT IN FAITH AND LET GOD
WORK MIRACLES THROUGH YOUR LIFE

Caroline Barnett
with A. J. Gregory

TYNDALE
MOMENTUM
An Imprint of Tyndale House Publishers, Inc.

Published in association with the literary agency of Fedd and Company, Inc., doing business at PO Box 341973, Austin, TX 78734.

Library of Congress Cataloging-in-Publication Data

Barnett, Caroline.
    Willing to walk on water : step out in faith and let God work miracles through your life / Caroline Barnett, with A.J. Gregory.
        pages cm
    Includes bibliographical references.
    ISBN 978-1-4143-7229-7 (pbk.)
    1. Faith. 2. Trust in God—Christianity. 3. Fear—Religious aspects—Christianity. 4. Church work. I. Title.
    BV4637.B298 2013
    248.4—dc23   2012049127

Printed in the United States of America

19	18	17	16	15	14	13
7	6	5	4	3	2	1

To Matthew and our two beautiful children,
Mia and Caden

Contents

Introduction

I AM, BY NATURE, a shy person who is perfectly content serving in the background. I never had a desire to speak publicly or preach from a pulpit. In fact, I ran from such things for the first ten years I was in full-time ministry. I wanted to throw up whenever Matthew, my husband, asked me to stand up front and simply greet the congregation. Once on stage, I would tremble like an exercise Shake Weight.

But not anymore. Now I can stand confidently in front of a crowd of people to tell my story or share God's message.

The change didn't happen overnight. But it did require a simple understanding of God's plan for me. I had to stand and speak to others in order to do the work I knew He was calling me to do in my community. And I was *willing* to do whatever it took.

It is with such willingness that I approach my ministry today. I am humbled by how God has used me and countless others to make the Dream Center a place where lives are changed for His glory. I am humbled by how He has blessed my own life. These were the driving factors behind my desire to write this book.

What I've learned is that once we make ourselves available to God, we can make a difference in the world's brokenness (no matter how large or small the problem we take on). When we act within God's plans for our lives and are open to taking a risk, we can make a positive impact on social injustice through service.

I didn't always think of service and social justice this way. As with most things, God had to open my eyes to see the connection between my life's work and His work. Even though I had been in ministry for years, I always assumed that our best efforts would only scratch the surface of the problems in our communities and in the world. The problems were just too big. Many times I felt like I was trying to save a sinking ship by scooping out the water one Dixie cup at a time.

I had no expectation or hope that the work I did alongside others could eliminate certain social injustices. I couldn't see that I was, in fact, a part of God's answer to the world's problems. And then God began to teach me about Himself and His purpose for my life. I began enlisting supporters for the Dream Center's women's ministry. What God had put on my heart to accomplish needed an army to make it happen. And sure enough, just over five years later, what our women's ministry has accomplished is remarkable. You'll read about this amazing ride throughout this book.

One of the key stories from the Bible that God used to prepare me is found in Matthew 14. Jesus' disciples are caught in a storm in the middle of a lake, fearfully battling strong winds, waves, and rain. Then Jesus shows up in a most unbelievable way.

About three o'clock in the morning Jesus came toward them, walking on the water. When the disciples saw him walking on the water, they were terrified. In their fear, they cried out, "It's a ghost!"

But Jesus spoke to them at once. "Don't be afraid," he said. "Take courage. I am here!"

Then Peter called to him, "Lord, if it's really you, tell me to come to you, walking on the water."

"Yes, come," Jesus said.

So Peter went over the side of the boat and walked on the water toward Jesus.

MATTHEW 14:25-29

Even though he is terrified, Peter takes Jesus at His word and literally walks out his faith with courage—courage to climb out of the boat. I feel God wants us to do the same thing. He wants us to face our fears and do the seemingly impossible. What it requires is desire and availability.

In his description of the same scene, the Gospel writer Mark adds a stunning piece of information. He recounts that Jesus "saw that they [the disciples] were in serious trouble, rowing hard and struggling against the wind and waves. About three o'clock in the morning Jesus came toward them, walking on the water. *He intended to go past them*" (Mark 6:48, emphasis added). As I meditated on this passage I couldn't get the sentence "He intended to go past them" out of my mind.

Jesus knew the disciples were in trouble. And yet although they struggled in the storm, none of them cried out to Him for help. As they unsuccessfully scuffled with the elements, pitting their puny human efforts against raging winds and crashing waves, one thing was clear: they couldn't do it on their own. They weren't strong or capable enough. The storm overpowered them. In His mercy, Jesus moved closer to them. But He waited until they called out to Him before He intervened. Had they not cried out for His help, I believe He would have walked past them.

God Wants to Use You

This walking-on-water illustration is applicable to us today. God knows the world is in trouble; the news is full of it every morning. If you're like me, when you hear about people in need, you deeply desire to get involved or take a stand. But we rarely act on those feelings, right? When we hear stories about modern-day slavery, sex trafficking, hunger issues, homelessness, or child abandonment, do we stop and say to God, "Show me how to solve this problem"? No, we don't.

But we should.

God wants to use us. However, He won't force ministry or a life of service on anyone. What He will do is partner with us and make it possible for us to find solutions to the problems plaguing our communities the world over. We just have to be willing to do the work. We can get it done if we trust God and follow His plan.

I believe if every Christian in the world were willing to make a positive change, we would make a significant impact in remedying and mending the brokenness that runs rampant in our local and global communities. The numbers are in our favor.

According to the most recent *Atlas of Global Christianity*, there are 2.2 billion Christians (that's a third of the world's population) and 4,850,000 congregations in the world.[1] With an army this large, is any problem insurmountable? Some people may look at the statistics and say it is.

> ▸ The Food and Agriculture Organization of the United Nations estimates that a total of 925 million people in the world go hungry.[2] Every day almost 16,000 children die from hunger-related causes.[3]

CAROLINE BARNETT

- An estimated 12 to 27 million people are caught in some form of slavery. Between 600,000 and 800,000 people in the world are victims of human trafficking.[4]
- 18.5 million children around the world have no parental care.[5]

No matter how overwhelming the amount of suffering or number of people in need all over the world, I believe that we, the Christian army, led and empowered by the Creator of the universe, can overcome these atrocities. Sure, it will take effort. It may take getting involved in the government's efforts or galvanizing a team of people or starting an organization. It may mean joining forces with the many Christian organizations around the world that have already started conquering these issues. It may require something as simple as sending a few dollars to a charity or knocking on the door of someone in your neighborhood who needs help. But all it initially requires is your willingness.

Lasting Rewards
For me, living my life with eyes and heart open to God's leading has brought fulfillment and joy. It has deepened and increased my faith. It has helped me focus less on my insecurities and on what I lack, and more on Jesus and what He can do through me. It has taught me about the love of God on a personal level. And it has resulted in countless miracles for those we have reached.

I know God has the same desire for your life. He wants you to change the world and make a strong impact in the particular area of injustice that speaks to your heart, whether it's helping the poor, feeding the hungry, adopting a child, preaching to the lost, healing the sick, mentoring a troubled youth, helping out a single mother, or teaching basic life skills to someone who needs them.

It doesn't matter who you are or what you do. Whether you're a pastor, a "domestic engineer," a student, or a CEO, God wants to use your willingness to do great things simply because you are His child and it's your responsibility to help to run the family business. He wants to ignite in you a passion to start doing something about the brokenness in the world.

My hope is that after reading this book, you will become convinced that you are part of the miracle God is looking for to help change the world. I pray that whatever has held you back from taking that first step of action to walk on water—whether lies, insecurities, doubts, or fears—will be brought to light and shattered.

I've divided the book into three parts. I begin with my own journey into ministry and how God has helped me understand and define my missions for His Kingdom. Then we'll look at the roadblocks that cause people to hesitate to serve, and I'll suggest ways to get past them. Finally, I'll share several lessons that I have learned over the past ten years and how they could benefit you. Hopefully the stories, Scripture, and practical ideas will help you identify your unique passion for service and clarify what God asks of you.

Before getting started, consider these questions:

Do you think you're too inexperienced to make a difference?

Do you think you're too busy to make a time commitment? Does even considering it make you nervous?

Do you think you're past your prime and these issues
   are best left to a younger generation?
Do you feel you lack the necessary skills, education,
   or network to relieve social injustices?

If you answered yes to at least one of these questions, I hope you'll continue reading so God can begin to speak to your heart. When you couple your willingness to walk on water with God's desire to perform miracles in people's lives, an exciting and fulfilling future awaits you.
   Ready to start walking?

Caroline Barnett

PART I

DISCOVERING

*Preach the gospel at all times
and if necessary use words.*

FRANCIS OF ASSISI

WILLING

I was hungry, and you fed me. I was thirsty, and you gave me a drink.
I was a stranger, and you invited me into your home.
I was naked, and you gave me clothing. I was sick, and you cared for me.
I was in prison, and you visited me.

— MATTHEW 25:35-36 —

I COULDN'T HELP but notice their eyes—extremely made up, but empty. These scantily clad young women were selling their bodies on Sunset Boulevard in Hollywood. It seemed as if they had already sold their souls.

I had moved into the Dream Center as a full-time volunteer in the beginning of 1997, a few months after I turned eighteen. I wanted to focus on ministries that pulled at my heartstrings, so I volunteered on many different outreaches to find the right fit. I had heard about the prostitution outreach and wanted to see what that was like. The team headed to the streets every Friday and Saturday night. Volunteers met at the Dream Center parking lot at midnight to get instructions from the leader as well as an overview of what to expect, and then the team would drive toward Sunset Boulevard. Once there, they would spend a few hours praying with and encouraging the prostitutes.

I went on my first outreach a month or so after I moved on campus. There were about sixteen of us paired up, within sight of each other. It was 2 a.m. and the "night shift" was in full swing. As police sirens blared in the distance, the prostitutes leaned provocatively against streetlights or slowly cruised the sidewalks looking for their next trick of the night.

Our team, consisting of men and women, spread out to talk to as many of the women as we could. We handed out roses and told them they were beautiful and that God loved them. Some politely smiled, while others rolled their eyes, their hearts hardened by years on the streets. I realized that they were numb to the possibility of another kind of life. How could I convince them they were worth so much more? How could I make them understand they had a loving Creator who could heal their hurts and give them a future they could look forward to?

I started talking to one of the prostitutes and told her about the Dream Center and the opportunity she had to get off the streets. After leaving her with a flyer with more information about our program, I walked farther down the block and glanced toward the street. A car approached, slowing down right alongside me.

The driver leaned over, hungrily peering out of the front passenger's window. He assumed I was one of the working girls. We stared at each other for a second. He didn't say anything, just stared me up and down. The evil that washed over his face—the lust, the insatiable appetite for pleasure no matter the cost—radiated so much wickedness, it made me feel sick to my stomach. *Every night, hundreds of women get into the cars of these kinds of men.* I shuddered to think of the dangers that lurked on the streets. And my heart broke when I imagined the emotional decay that grows deeper after every trick turned. *It's no wonder these women feel hopeless.*

As a full-time volunteer at the Dream Center, serving in some of the worst communities in the heart of Los Angeles, I felt I was being faithful to God and His call on my life. I wasn't looking out only for me. I was following the apostle Paul's exhortation to "take an interest in others, too" (Philippians 2:4). I wasn't oblivious to the suffering that existed in the world. I was doing my part to change it. From ministering to prostitutes to feeding the homeless and building relationships with struggling youth in crime- and gang-infested neighborhoods, I was making a difference.

And then God opened my eyes.

Roots

My family had immigrated to California from Sweden in 1980, when I was two years old. My parents wanted to live the American dream of starting a Swedish crystal chandelier and area-rug business called Scandinavian Handicrafts. Before coming to the States, they had sold their home and invested all of their savings to buy the inventory for the store, which they had shipped from Sweden to America. My dad left a successful job with an insurance company to follow his dream. He was the youngest of four boys, so it was hard for him to leave behind his mother and siblings. Moving was also difficult for my mother; she didn't speak English and didn't know anything about American culture.

Though they started out hopeful, it became apparent that crystal chandeliers weren't hot sellers in the early 1980s. Eventually, my parents liquidated their inventory at swap meets. Times were tough. My dad took any job he could find to make ends meet, including working as a truck driver. Yet my parents never regretted their decision to move to the United States; they loved the freedom and opportunities America had to offer.

I grew up in a strong Christian home. My parents were very involved in church and volunteered for everything, from the worship team to children's church. My mom sewed all the costumes for the Christmas pageants as well as vests for the choir members singing in the Christmas cantata. She also helped with costumes for Easter-related sermons. And she was an incredible cook and baker who baked desserts for every event.

My parents always opened our home to Swedish missionaries and ministers passing through town, usually on their way to South America. It didn't matter that my parents, my three sisters, and I lived in a two-bedroom apartment. We loved having the missionaries stay with us. I was always fascinated with their stories and hearing my parents talk about their own experiences as traveling evangelists in Sweden.

Both my parents have worked for God their entire lives, while they were single and married. My dad had started traveling as an evangelist when he was sixteen years old. Once he got married and held a full-time job, he had to limit his time on the road. He did, however, continue to hold tent revivals, lead worship, and preach at his church while he lived in Sweden. My mom has been devoted to the church since she was a little girl and has always volunteered as much as she could.

Through their strong faith and their devotion to service, our parents taught my sisters and me to generously serve others for God. However, the thought of going into full-time ministry never crossed my mind when I was younger. Growing up in a family whose finances were always tight, all I wanted was to be successful in business.

I was a good student. I went to a public school and had lots of friends with different backgrounds. During my junior and senior years of high school I started going to parties, dancing, and drinking every now and then with my friends, some of whom were Christians. As a cheerleader, I partied with most of the girls on my squad. I'm not trying to justify my behavior, but I was just curious, having fun with my friends.

I still went to church regularly, attended youth group meetings, and participated in all the youth camps. My parents were unaware of my double life. When my friends invited me to a party, I would tell my parents that I was staying overnight at a friend's house. Mom and Dad trusted me and never gave it a second thought. Though I felt convicted and would repent to God privately afterward and at the end of every Sunday morning church service, I continued.

Is There Something More?

Toward the end of my senior year I began to change. The parties were getting old; I wasn't having as much fun. *There has to be more to life than this,* I thought. I started searching for answers in the Bible.

Reading the words of Jesus fired me up—I was intent on finding God's plan for my life. I ended up confessing to my dad about my partying habits and even asked him to ground me. He was more than happy to oblige. I didn't feel strong enough to say no to my friends and figured saying I was grounded was an easier way out. I stopped caring about the things that most of my former friends did, like worrying about what to wear or scoping out cute boys. Instead I focused on seeking the Kingdom of God (see Matthew 6:31-34). I was particularly moved by verse 32, which says that unbelievers tend to worry about day-to-day things. As I read the Gospels, I was inspired by the wonderful miracles Jesus performed and His commission to His disciples to further His Kingdom (Matthew 28:18-20).

Suddenly the things I had previously considered important didn't matter to me anymore. The thought of pursuing a business career seemed empty. I didn't want to have to work just so I could pay for a car, gas, food, and a place to live. I wanted something more. I remember praying, *God, I know You have given me a free will to have a dream, but all I want is to be Your hands and feet to find the lost and heal the sick and the broken-hearted. I don't have to have my own dream; I want to be a part of Your dream.*

Looking for a Place to Serve

I was hoping He was going to call me to serve Him somewhere exotic and far away. I couldn't wait to turn eighteen so I could leave Los Angeles. I hated the city at the time. We lived in an area where gang violence was rampant. As a matter of fact, the Rodney King riots occurred near our neighborhood. The high school I attended was also riddled with violence, most of the time racially motivated. There were many times when teachers were concerned some of my friends and I would be targets and hid us in a classroom if a riot broke out on the school grounds. I viewed Los Angeles as a city of limits. Life seemed such a struggle for most people, and it was hard to get ahead. I assumed it would be easier to make it anywhere else.

I passionately wanted to work for God, but I wasn't bold enough to preach the gospel on a street corner. I desperately wanted to make a difference for Christ and was frustrated because I didn't know *what* to do. Around this time two pastors from Norway came to stay with our family. They had heard about Los Angeles International Church and wanted to visit. My dad had never been there, so they all went and toured the facilities. When my dad came home, he was so inspired that he was beaming. (In 1996, the Los Angeles International Church became the Dream Center, named by the people on the streets because it was a place where they could start to dream again.)

Not long after my dad's visit, Pastor Matthew Barnett, one

of the founders of the Dream Center, spoke at our church. My mom knew about him and believed I would be inspired by all he was doing, especially since he was young. I went with a friend and was moved by Matthew's strong desire to rescue the spiritually lost and to help those in need. I remember telling my friend, "I could marry a man like that one day." She was shocked by my comment since I had never had a boyfriend, though I had been on a few dates. My friends always said I was too picky and joked that I would be single my whole life.

A month later I attended a Thursday night service at the Dream Center. It was my first time there, and as soon as I walked on campus I knew that was the place I was called to. It's hard to describe, but I had an incredible peace in my spirit that I was called to be a part of this organization. During the service and in later conversations with people who were part of the ministry, I discovered more about the work they were doing. They followed in the steps of Jesus, imitating His example through tangible acts of service. Everything I wanted to do was being done there. I had found an outlet for my passion to serve.

I started volunteering as much as I could. After I graduated from high school, my parents moved an hour away from Los Angeles, but the distance didn't stop me. I found a way to volunteer almost every day of the week. Every morning, I'd drive to work as a receptionist for Farmers Insurance, and after my workday, I'd drive over to the Dream Center. I'd volunteer for a few hours starting at around six thirty in the evening until about ten. More and more, I couldn't wait to finish my job in order to get to the Dream Center to help any way I could. Within a couple of months, I was offered a full-time volunteer position, so I resigned from my insurance job and the Dream Center became my new home.

My heart longed to minister to people on the streets, but I wanted to start serving immediately, so I wrote on my application, "Put me wherever you need me." The Dream Center was an exciting place to be in the early years, a place of beautiful chaos. In the beginning, our team was unseasoned and not as organized as we are today. Though we had much growing and learning to do, we made up for it with passion. There were about two hundred different ministries running simultaneously—from the residential programs to help people get back on their feet from homelessness, addictions, prostitution, and depression, to the various street outreaches. Our radar was always tuned to different needs in the community. We were itching to help where we could. Our zealousness helped spur many new ministries—some worked, others didn't.

I wore many hats when I started out, mainly working in the business office, doing a little bit of everything—helping each ministry define its mission statement, meeting with people to brainstorm new ideas for ministries, planning events, giving tours of the facilities to potential donors. Wherever there was a need, I plugged myself in. I worked in our accounting department, our registration office, and the reception area. I chopped vegetables for meals, helped put on neighborhood carnivals, and organized church services in our local convalescent home every Sunday afternoon.

When I came on board, 350 people lived on campus: 100 volunteers working with 250 people in the programs. Today, 700 people call the Dream Center home: 115 interns, 75 staff members, 40 graduates from our programs who volunteer to give back, and 470 men, women, and children who are getting help for a particular need. The need keeps growing.

Over the last sixteen years, I have seen so many hurting people. I have smelled the acrid stench of urine and feces that permeates downtown crack hotels. I have delivered thousands of bags of food to families at risk of malnourishment. I have served hot meals to people dying of AIDS and later helped make funeral arrangements for them. I have spent nights on street corners reaching out to prostitutes hardened by years of abuse. I have spent time in skid row, inviting people to church and building relationships with kids who have witnessed murders, who have seen victims of drug overdoses, and who have been regularly raped themselves.

I wasn't naive. I saw firsthand the oppression, darkness, and brokenness that evil casts in this world. And I knew I was helping in some way. Working with the different ministry teams, I was doing my part. We were making a difference.

Yet God was about to take me to the next level. He was about to challenge and change my entire perspective on making a difference, on serving others, and specifically on working in the arena of social justice.

Turning Point

In early 2000, there was a strong push from people in our church to start a women's conference. I personally had no desire to do it, but I decided to attend some other women's conferences to learn more. In 2006 I attended the Colour Conference led by Bobbie Houston and the Hillsong Church in Australia. More than 30,000 women attended. It was spectacular and so motivating! One of the highlights was seeing the documentary *Invisible Children*.

The film focuses on the twenty-year civil war in Uganda that has destroyed the lives of hundreds of thousands of that country's children through abduction, torture, and even murder. Thousands of the "lucky" ones who evaded capture fled the country and spent the rest of their young lives on the run—homeless, hungry, and alone.

I cried through the hour-long documentary. It wasn't because I hadn't seen extreme brokenness in my work at the Dream Center. But now, for the first time, I sensed the evil that permeated not just the dark corners of one African country but the global community as a whole. *The world is beyond wicked,* I thought. I felt heartbroken and defeated. It seemed the devil was winning the war on souls, and I didn't feel like God was doing anything about it.

That night I couldn't sleep. I tossed and turned, haunted by the images I had seen on-screen. The ten-year-old boys tearfully talking about the murder of their parents, their eyes full of pain, remembering. The hundreds of children hiding from rebels in dark, damp basements, so closely packed together they could barely breathe. The lifeless eyes of the kids who had given up, who were tired of running.

I'll be honest. I was mad at God. "Why are You letting this happen?" I cried out. "Why aren't You doing something? Why don't You care?"

In the depths of my spirit, I heard His gentle reply. His words weren't shaming or condemning. They overflowed with love. *Caroline, I sent My Son, Jesus, to pay for the sin of what you just saw so that there would be hope for redemption. I sent My Son, Jesus, to pay for the healing that will need to take place. In My Word I have promised to provide and to protect. I have done and given you everything you need to change it. So, Caroline, why are you allowing this to happen?*

Though I wasn't compelled to start a women's conference after I got home from the event, I was inspired to start a women's ministry and to accomplish the things God would orchestrate.

It's Our Problem

I was stunned and needed time to process what God had said. I had so many questions and was overwhelmed with conflicting emotions. In essence, I felt that God was saying that the devastation documented in the film was my fault. I couldn't get that idea out of my head. Was I, were we as Christians, partially or even fully responsible for not preventing the wrongs being done in the world? And if so, what was I supposed to do about it?

I had been working nonstop in my own community for nine years. Besides, I was just one person. What difference could I possibly make, especially in a place as far away as Uganda? Weren't those monumental issues the responsibility of governments and global organizations to deal with? I was anxious for God to explain it further.

After seeing the documentary, I began to look at the world immediately around me, the people in my own backyard. I could clearly see we were surrounded by social injustices that hindered people from reaching their full God-given potential. But where to begin?

The Power of God's Word

I picked up my Bible and started reading the stories of Moses, Joshua, Gideon, and others—ordinary people who accomplished audacious feats for God, empowered by His Spirit.

Later that week, I shared what I was reading with my hairdresser while she worked her magic on my hair. Describing how God intervened in people's lives, I asked her, "Do you believe God can do those kinds of miracles today to save His children?" Pausing for a minute, she answered, "Well, maybe not literally, like in the Bible."

Her words struck me. One of God's biggest frustrations

must be how lightly some of us interpret the Bible, thinking of His Word as merely a storybook filled with moral lessons to follow and teach our kids. *Obey your parents. Do unto others. Turn the other cheek.* The Bible, however, is filled with stories of how God, through one person, made the impossible happen. And He wants to do the same thing through us.

It's time for us to live out our lives like we believe God's Word with all our heart, soul, and mind. We must study and apply His promises every day. We must use the Bible as a guide to living the abundant life He has intended for us. God may not duplicate the same biblical miracles we read about, but He can and does perform new ones.

I believe there is no limit to what God will do to save His children. There is no prayer so great that He cannot answer it. There is no injustice so overpowering that He cannot put it right. God can bring healing to our souls and our bodies.

Discovering the Secret

While I was excited about the truths God was stirring in my soul and encouraged by the Scriptures that showed His faithfulness and provision, I still didn't see how all this applied directly to alleviating social problems today.

That is, until I started studying the book of Exodus and came to chapter 35.

Moses called the people of Israel together and explained that God wanted them to build a dwelling place for Him in the wilderness, His Tabernacle. Issuing specific instructions through Moses, God used every individual to accomplish His will; everyone had something to offer.

Moses asked the people to give whatever material possessions they could—items like linens, oils, and spices (verses 5-9). Most households could contribute something. Moses also called for volunteers, "gifted craftsmen" (verse 10), to help in the actual construction of the Tabernacle, whether making tent pegs, curtains, or the altar. God wanted experienced men and women, but also any and everyone who was willing to help carry out His plan.

And come they did. "All whose hearts were stirred and whose spirits were moved came and brought their sacred offerings to the LORD. . . . Both men and women came, all whose hearts were willing" (verses 21 and 22).

Not only did these people give and do what they were commanded, they were so inspired that they "continued to bring additional gifts" (Exodus 36:3). Eventually, Moses had to tell the community to stop giving because there were more than enough materials to finish the entire project. Isn't that amazing? And it happens today, too. When people who are willing to give come through and those who are willing to do spring into action, miracles happen. The key is willingness.

Be Someone's Miracle

It finally clicked for me. God is looking for *willing* people He can use to do life- and even world-changing things. I love what my husband, Matthew, says: "Find a need and fill it." Serve others and make a difference. The Bible mentions helping the poor and needy 358 times. And yet we don't need to wait for God's approval or His confirmation to relieve injustice and the burdens of others. We just need to begin somewhere.

If you are willing to use your time, your efforts, your resources (limited or unlimited), you can be a walking-on-water miracle to another person. From there, it may grow into affecting an entire community.

Here's how simply it can begin. What are you planning to

have for dinner tonight? If you don't plan a weekly menu in advance, you may spend a few minutes deciding between one choice or another. Now think about the single mother who is out of work, who has no money and empty cupboards. What are her options? If you showed up at her home with a prepared dinner and a bag of groceries for a few more, don't you think she'd consider your generosity a miracle?

How about a young man with a troubled past who has always felt neglected and unloved? Hopefully, your experience has been the exact opposite—your parents have encouraged you all your life. What a miracle it would be for that young man to be mentored by someone who loves him and speaks life and truth into his soul. Imagine the amount of self-worth and possibilities of a better future that can be birthed from that relationship, as well as the multiplying effect for generations to come through this young man's offspring.

Once you experience the thrill of being God's hands and feet to someone in need, you will look for more and more opportunities. Your reward? Indescribable joy.

The Truth about "Good Works"
Our willingness is more than enough to accomplish God's will. So what's His will for us today? Many people spend their entire lives trying to figure it out. First and foremost, God desires that every human being accept His gift of salvation. John 3:16 tells us that God does not want anyone to perish but to have eternal life. First Timothy 2:3-4 says, "This is good and pleases God our Savior, who wants everyone to be saved and to understand the truth."

When Jesus died on the cross for our sins, He reconciled us with God and gave us an example to follow. Jesus lived a life of service, showing and giving love, grace, and mercy to others. We are called to do the same—to use our time, resources, and talents to build His church, the body of Christ—you and I and everyone who is added to God's family by the work that we do.

I want to make one thing clear: doing your part to help the needy, the hungry, and the oppressed isn't your ticket to earning salvation. You're not going to get to heaven because you helped a family in need. Being willing to make a difference is not about tallying religious brownie points or doing enough good deeds to be considered worthy enough to be saved.

Also, God will not love you any more or any less if you help the poor or if you don't. His love for you has always been complete and perfect—before and after you were saved, before and after your mistakes, even whether you are obedient or not.

Despite my best efforts at living a Christian life, I had a hard time accepting grace. I didn't understand that I didn't have to keep asking God to forgive me for the same things I had asked forgiveness for a day, a week, or a month ago. While we have to constantly live in a place of repentance because we sin every day, we don't need to repent for the same sin we've already repented for.

For a year, after every church service at the Dream Center, I'd go forward and tearfully ask God to forgive me for things I had already asked him to forgive.

Finally, I felt the Lord speak to my heart.

Caroline, are you done yet?

"Oh, God, I just need You to forgive me."

I forgave you the first time you asked.

"But I need You to see how sorry I am."

Are you trying to earn your salvation, Caroline?

Well, yes, I was. I was trying to punish myself enough to

feel I had the right to be forgiven. Receiving God's grace and being saved, forgiven, and accepted is not something that makes much sense. But that's how much God loves us. We don't need to prove our worthiness to Him. Because Jesus became our sacrificial substitute, God accepts us in our unworthiness. He is merciful toward us. And He forgives us.

That incredible gift is worth sharing.

How to Begin

Throughout this book I'll share stories—my own experiences as well as those of others who are committed to serving those in need.

You might be wondering where you can start. Remember, you are not responsible for changing the entire world or doing grand acts of service. Every bit of willingness matters to God.

Just to spark your own thinking, here are some simple yet life-changing ideas you can consider putting into practice:

- Babysit for a single mom. It's amazing how even a few hours will refresh her.
- Make dinner for a family in need in your neighborhood.
- If you have couponing skills, go grocery shopping. Donate both the money you save and the items you buy to a local food pantry.
- Mow the lawn of a widow who just lost her husband.
- Invite a struggling teenager from your church or community to a fun activity.
- Offer rides to the grocery store or medical appointments for someone who has no car.
- Plan a Christmas or holiday party for kids in an impoverished neighborhood.

- Take someone with little means out for a birthday celebration.
- Ask someone if you can pray for his or her specific need.
- Help a tired mom clean and organize her house.
- Make care packages for troops overseas.
- Plant flowers in a neighbor's yard or in a window box to give the person something beautiful to look at.

If you feel called to make a greater commitment that may require more time, here are other ideas:

- Become a mentor.
- Hold a neighborhood food drive.
- If you have a vegetable garden, share your bounty.
- Regularly prepare, deliver, and serve meals to families.
- Apply for a license to become an honorary aunt or uncle to a foster child so you can babysit or provide other care as needed. Your experience may possibly lead you to consider adoption in the future.
- Donate your skills to help someone who can't afford to hire a plumber, house cleaner, or handyman.
- Volunteer at a local organization such as a soup kitchen, youth center, or homeless shelter.
- Grab some trash bags and help clean up a local neighborhood.
- Raise funds for an organization to help victims of a particular injustice such as human trafficking.

Do you see a common thread running through these ideas? They work only if you know there is a need to begin with. That means you need to listen, be observant, respect people's privacy, and not give up if your request is turned down. When you start looking for opportunities to serve, you'll be surprised at how many times opportunity will knock.

I hope the excitement is beginning to build in your mind and heart. You may still wonder if it's even possible for you to walk on water. Let me encourage you. Yes, it's possible. And yes, you can. The God who parted the Red Sea is the same God whose Spirit lives inside you and empowers you. The God who fed a crowd of five thousand people with merely five loaves and two fish is the same God whose Spirit lives inside you and empowers you. The God who brought Jesus back to life after He was in the tomb for three days is the same God whose Spirit lives inside you and empowers you. You are asked only to be willing to go and do what God is asking of you. You are the hero He is looking for to partner with Him.

You no longer have to look at our world and be brought to tears by the devastation, as I was when learning about the plight of child soldiers in Uganda. You don't have to look at injustices and turn away because it hurts too much or you feel powerless to do anything about it. You no longer have to live with the fear of what the world will bring to your children and your children's children.

Everyone's willingness put into action will look different. Some may volunteer for a cause. Some may create an organization to fill a need. Some may lead a particular movement. You are not called to serve others on the same level that someone else is. You are required only to be willing to go or do what God is asking of *you*. When we position ourselves in the body of Christ in this way, the problems of this world don't look so overwhelming anymore.

Are you willing to go?

Are you willing to take a step forward?
Are you willing to never look back?

If you are willing to say yes, I guarantee that God will give you whatever you need to accomplish the task.

CHAPTER 2

WHAT'S YOUR TRIGGER?

Share each other's burdens, and in this way obey the law of Christ.

—— GALATIANS 6:2 ——

IT WAS A SPRING DAY in 1997 and I was helping out in the Dream Center reception office when the phone rang. A social worker on the other end told me about a family in need living only a few blocks away from us. I thanked her, then called my best friend from Sweden, Sara, who had recently flown in to volunteer at the Dream Center for a year, and asked her to meet me at the campus food pantry. Together we packed and bagged bread, fresh produce, and some canned goods into three boxes, loaded them into my 1978 diesel Volvo station wagon, and headed to the address the social worker had given me.

I drove slowly down the street, passing one dilapidated apartment building after another. They had broken windows and cracked siding, and their roofs looked on the verge of collapsing, every one of them in need of repair. Lawns were littered with broken beer bottles, mounds of dog feces, and half-eaten *elotes* (corn on the cob in the husk sold from nearby street carts). There were no grassy areas for the kids to play on, just random patches of crumbling cement and dead plants in unattended containers. From one apartment, the music blared so loudly you could hear it down the entire street. Every time I saw such an impoverished neighborhood, it broke my heart, but it wasn't as shocking to me as it was to my friend.

Finally we arrived. When I knocked on the door, it opened with a loud creaking sound. There stood a weary mother, smiling faintly. My heart tumbled as I quickly counted eight children clothed only in underwear or diapers huddled around her, their eyes wide and curious. The smell from inside the room hit me full force—sweaty bodies and unchanged diapers. I sensed it had been a long time since anyone had had a bath. As tired and ragged as the woman looked, she couldn't have been much older than twenty-five.

Once the kids spotted the boxes of food we carried, a few of them gasped in amazement, some even leapt into our arms, practically knocking us over. I accidentally dropped one of the bags in the commotion, and a handful of produce plummeted to the floor. One of the children grabbed a zucchini that was rolling down the dirt-covered hallway and excitedly shoved it in her mouth, taking noisy bites with her brown-stained teeth. *A raw zucchini?* I thought. *Many kids refuse to eat cooked vegetables at all, no matter how tasty, and this little girl is devouring one with hardly any taste at all! How long has it been since they've had anything to eat?*

The apartment was practically bare, with linoleum floors that were cracked and filthy. The foam stuffing was coming out of the couch cushions that littered the living room. My guess was that the cushions doubled as the children's beds. The only things in the kitchen cupboards were dead bugs. *Children live here,* I grieved to myself, *little children. This should not be happening. Not in the richest country in the world.*

All eight kids followed and surrounded us, so close on our heels it was hard not to trip over or bump into them. They clamored around us, sixteen outstretched arms desperately grabbing at anything we tried to put on the shelves. It was a madhouse. I felt fingers gripping and shaking my arms, trying to knock a loaf of bread out of my hand. These kids were hungry. Only God knew the last time they had had a proper meal.

My Trigger

What I saw that day changed my life. It was my trigger, one that created in me a passion to make a change and take action. I walked away from that apartment knowing I couldn't sit back and do nothing about the hunger problem that ravaged impoverished families and children.

I did have a foundation to build upon—the Dream Center's food bank. It had been one of the first ministries created to meet an immediate need. We originally opened the food bank on campus to the public on certain days. The need was so great, however, that people would show up on any day of the week asking for food. We never turned anyone away and would serve whoever came, but also let them know to come back at particular times.

The ministry was providing a vital service, but I realized we could turn something good into something great. A large percentage of the people who needed food had no way to get to the food bank. They didn't have cars or money for public transportation. If we were going to maximize our ministry, we needed to get to the people who couldn't get to us. We needed to be proactive and meet them where they lived, not merely serve those who showed up on our doorstep. God was beginning to unfold a plan in my mind: a mobile food-bank ministry.

With the heartbreaking scene at the apartment still fresh in my mind, I sat down with Pastor Matthew and described what I had seen. He gave me the green light to start a mobile food-bank ministry. (I called my future husband Pastor Matthew before we started dating and even during the beginning of our courtship. I figured if our relationship didn't work out, it would make it easier to switch back to calling him Pastor.)

After receiving the go-ahead, I paused to reflect on how God works. A few months earlier, I would have laughed at even considering the idea, let alone spearheading it. It wasn't something that interested me. Oh, I recognized that hunger is a severe problem worldwide. I had grown up watching hundreds of television spots showing starving kids in third-world countries with bulging bellies and vacant eyes. Though the images moved me to tears, they never propelled me toward action. I would simply change the channel or turn off the TV.

My outlook shifted, however, when I stood in the midst of eight emaciated children in my neighborhood, begging for a cracker, a chip, a raw vegetable, or a piece of fruit—anything to curb the hunger pangs that throbbed in their bellies. They were my trigger.

What about you? What injustice grips your heart the most? Is it crack babies, orphaned toddlers whose lives have been confined to cribs, AIDS victims who can't afford treatment, children whose innocence has been stolen by sex traffickers? Maybe it's a single mother you've met who barely sees her children because she is working three jobs and still struggles to pay the bills. Being sympathetic shows you have a heart. But having sympathy and taking a step forward to effect change are two different things. When you are triggered by a particular injustice, your compassion doesn't end with a few shed tears. It leads to action.

Finding Your Trigger

God has made each one of us unique. I believe that's why our hearts break over different causes. I may feel a pull toward helping orphans in the foster-care system, while you feel motivated to be an advocate for the homeless in your community. Whether your passion is drug-addicted youth, providing clean water for a village in a third-world country, or teaching adults how to read, God has placed a unique area of compassion within your heart to be sparked and set aflame.

Here are some starting points that will help you determine your own trigger:

- Research an area of injustice that infuriates you.
- Volunteer at an existing organization to see if it seems the right fit.
- Think about what you are naturally good at and enjoy doing, and translate that into acts of service. If you're computer savvy, you might consider tutoring teens who are struggling or single moms who need to go back into the workplace. If you're athletic, you can volunteer at a youth center and coach a team.
- If you are a visionary and want to see legislative changes, rather than protesting against a certain bill or law, start providing solutions and working models to show how a biblically based approach is even more effective.
- Is there an area you have purposely avoided? Consider revisiting it. Sometimes what we run from is exactly what God calls us to do.
- Determine what your comfort zone is and challenge yourself to step outside of it. It will stretch your "walking-on-water" faith.

▸ Prayerfully ask God for guidance and enlist at least one other person to intercede on your behalf for this purpose.

I've learned that sometimes you need to dig deep to know what moves you enough to want to do something about it. Don't distance yourself from the problem by just watching a video, looking at pictures, or reading an article. Spend time in the trenches. Smell the odors. Feel the fears. Taste the bitterness. Hear the cries. Hug the unloved and unlovely. See things with your own eyes. When you invest time in a world different from your own, it gives you perspective. And perspective often ignites passion. Once that passion is ignited by God, it will be fanned into a roaring fire that will compel you to take action. Two women I know found that to be true.

Finding a Trigger through Willingness
Kelli ultimately found her trigger when she met a pregnant eighteen-year-old girl.

> Several years ago I was overseeing the children's ministry at the Dream Center. I connected with a family from one of our Adopt-A-Block sites and began picking up the four siblings several times a week for church services and activities. Their father was in prison and their mother was a drug addict. The children were in and out of homeless shelters and had very little stability in their lives outside of the church. I met their eighteen-year-old sister when she was seven and a half months pregnant. Her mom had kicked her out of the house and she literally had nowhere to go.

I was in my early twenties, single and living in a
two-bedroom apartment, so I invited her to come and
live with me. She and her baby girl ended up staying
for almost two years. During that time I did my best to
show her Christ and help her in whatever way I could.
However, I made a lot of mistakes. I wasn't a mother and
had never dealt with homelessness or drug addiction.
There were many times when I felt it was all just too
much for me. Here I was, basically raising a baby and a
teenager at the same time, and I had absolutely no idea
what I was doing.

I had no choice but to lean on God for His wisdom
and help. He showed me 2 Corinthians 1:3-4: "Blessed
be the God and Father of our Lord Jesus Christ,
the Father of mercies and God of all comfort, who
comforts us in all our tribulation, that we may be able
to comfort those who are in any trouble, with the
comfort with which we ourselves are comforted by
God" (NKJV).

I realized that I didn't have to be a single mom to
help a single mom. Single parents held a special place in
my heart. A few years later Pastor Matthew and Caroline
would ask me to open and run a transitional housing
program for homeless families.

God was able to use my willingness and turn my
inexperience into preparation for His later calling on my
life. Today, over seven years later, that girl and her now
three children are still important people in my life, and
I have the added privilege of helping thirty families get
back on their feet.

Finding a Trigger through Obedience

Danise is proof that simply being obedient to God's call can turn a doubting heart into a willing heart. She decided to take God at His word, remain faithful, and trust Him, despite other people's strong opinions to the contrary and her own initial discomfort and concerns.

In 2001 our family faced a season of change. After serving in the same local church for fourteen years, our family felt called by God to leave our suburban comfort zone to serve at the Dream Center. This meant commuting nearly eighty miles round trip multiple times a week and leaving a church family we loved. There were many emotional reasons to stay and really only one reason to go—obedience to God. So we went, with the blessing of our church pastor.

Our first Sunday service at the Dream Center was a culture shock for me. We arrived at church, located in one of the most challenged neighborhoods of Los Angeles. I looked around at the congregation and noticed there weren't any other families. My children were sitting next to a group of homeless men who had been bused in from skid row. We stuck out like a sore thumb in our new environment—a suburban home-schooling family who didn't fit in.

For a moment my mind was flooded with doubt. I heard the voices of all the people who were skeptical of our decision: "How can you expose your children to the devastation and dangers of the inner city?" "It's great to have a heart for the needy . . . but is it really responsible to bring your children to a place like that?" "Aren't you afraid of getting shot!?" I quickly refocused my thoughts on God to find His peace. I was uncomfortable in my new surroundings, but strangely, I also felt like I was home.

During week two, I had a personal meltdown. Pastor Matthew's sermon was wonderful, but I was miserable. After the service I escaped into the restroom, relieved to find no one around. I couldn't stop the tears. I looked at myself in the mirror and said, "This was a BIG mistake! What do you have to offer to anyone here? Our children don't belong here . . . you don't belong here!" Just as quickly as the words came out of my mouth, deep in my heart I heard God remind me, *You belong to Me. You belong wherever I send you.*

That day, God filled my heart with a deeper compassion for people. Not long after, Caroline asked me to start a women's Bible study, which led to my becoming a mentor. It is such a joy to bring smiles and hope to women who have experienced deep pain and discouragement.

Walking the First Steps

Back to my own story. As energized as I was when I found my trigger, I had a lot of work to do to make it a reality. Even though I had served in many different areas on campus, I had spent very little time with the food ministry that provided for both campus residents and the homeless. I tried to learn everything I could about the way the food bank was managed.

I became the director of the food truck ministry in March of 1998. Though I spent most of my time working out the logistics, I continued to help out in other departments in the Dream Center when time allowed. We started serving the public immediately, though it took a few months before we were able to meet the demand. Along the way, I learned many valuable lessons.

> *It's important to keep volunteers happy and enthusiastic so they'll want to continue serving.* I found that they took pride and satisfaction in being used to accomplish something for God. If they felt they were making a positive difference, they wanted to serve and sacrifice even more.

> *You have to be creative with the volunteers you have.* We didn't always have the same number of volunteers at the Dream Center. Sometimes I had fewer than I needed; other times I had more than enough. So depending on how many people showed up, I had to either ask people we knew in the community to help out our team or use the surplus of volunteers to do other jobs within the community.

> *Match personality types with jobs.* I found this allowed the most efficient use of volunteers. For instance, I used the more vocal, outgoing volunteers to pray for the people we were serving and the shyer types to bag food in the truck.

> *There will always be a few complainers.* While the majority of people we served were wonderful, there were always a few we could never make happy. I learned it was better to focus on the people who needed and appreciated our efforts. It wasn't that I ignored the folks who were negative. At first, I tried to change their attitudes and win them over, but time and time again, there was no change. I was just wasting my energy. My time was better spent on people with open hearts.

It wasn't long before I hit my first snag. I realized that our existing food bank's supply wasn't adequate for the people we were already feeding, let alone expanding its reach with the food truck. I had to figure out a way to significantly increase our donations.

I made some phone calls. I networked like crazy. I did everything I could to galvanize support and resources from donors, grocery stores, food distributors, other local food banks, and farms.

It was a daunting task, but I believed that if God put the need on my heart, He would make it possible to feed all these people. He would somehow provide enough food to restock the supply we depleted each week. During that time, I learned about His provision. All of the suppliers we connected with gave us first dibs on food because we were on time to pick up the donations and we were committed. When we showed up, we found food.

Though we had over a hundred different contacts that would provide food once a month or year, we had about ten suppliers who consistently gave us food on a weekly basis. Our contacts also referred us to other potential donors, which provided a wonderful snowball effect. Sometimes, however, the logistics of picking up the food was tricky. We would get calls that required an immediate pickup or we would lose the donation. Once the food bank expanded, however, certain staff members were designated to solely handle the acquisitions, and I was able to step back and focus on the ministry outreach side.

It wasn't long before our box truck was too small to pick up, store, and redistribute all the food. The Dream Center invested in a very old, very used semitruck to keep up with our ever-expanding food supply.

God's Food Truck

We were growing rapidly. The more food we received, the more the food bank expanded. The bigger the food bank, the more staff we needed. The food truck ministry alone involved three young women under the age of twenty, myself included. None of us could drive the truck because we weren't old enough to be added to the church's insurance policy. I frequently enlisted my beautiful and charming friend Sara to find someone on campus who was willing to drive the truck for us that day. With her magnetic personality, finding a driver was never a problem.

It took a lot of effort, hard work, and a few adjustments along the way, but eventually everything fell into place. Within the first week of our launch, our first box truck was donated. We used this truck in the mornings to pick up food, usually an entire truckload of one item, like loaves of bread. We would then head back to the Dream Center, unload all of the bread, and then determine what was available in the main food bank that we could use for the off-site runs that day. We'd choose anywhere from five to ten different grocery items and pack enough to feed two hundred families.

We continued to stock up the main food bank by making pickups where needed. The joint effort between the original food bank and the food truck ministry attracted more contacts and bolstered our donations.

Our food supply was different each week. It was exciting because we never knew what was coming in. We are so grateful for the USDA's contribution of staples like peanut butter, canned tuna, beans, rice, and dry milk. Most of our fresh produce came from local farmers, and on occasion, members of the community would donate baby supplies. Angelus Temple, a church located a short distance away from our campus, gave us whatever was left over each week from their food bank's supply.

During the first month of our ministry, our team picked five sites in at-risk neighborhoods to visit on a weekly basis. Specifically targeting families, we strategically set up shop across from the elementary school in each community, arriving right before school ended for the day. We prepared three to five bags of groceries to donate to each family. At first, only a handful of curious parents came. But I underestimated what word-of-mouth promotion can do.

Within a matter of weeks, two hundred families were lining up for blocks at our five different sites. Our truck became a fixture in the neighborhoods. Three months after we started the ministry, we were able to bless a total of a thousand families per week. Some began bringing shopping carts to make it easier to get the bags home. The people were so grateful, you'd think we were giving away pots of gold.

Love and Prayers

I truly enjoy being around the people we serve. They are some of the kindest and warmest people I have ever met. When I pass out bags of groceries, I look into the eyes of every individual and am reminded that I'm not just handing a bag to a stranger in need—I'm handing a bag to Jesus. In Matthew 25, Jesus explains how serving others is actually serving Him. "I tell you the truth, when you did it to one of the least of these my brothers and sisters, you were doing it to me!" (verse 40).

One of my favorite parts of the food truck ministry is the opportunity we have to pray for the people waiting in line. We never preach or force our faith on anyone. We simply walk down the line and ask every person if they have a need they would like us to pray for. Almost everyone says yes.

There are always a slew of requests, like prayers for healing or help in dealing with a rebellious teenager. But most of the requests center on provision. These folks need help to survive on their own. They don't ask for a handout, for money to grow on trees, or for winning lottery numbers. They pray for work. And we pray wholeheartedly that God opens the door of employment and opportunity for them.

The Great Multiplier

One day my eyes were riveted on the hordes of people who had been waiting in line for hours for groceries. Some clutched antsy children and held crying infants. The need for food was so great. Suddenly, I was overcome with fear. *How long can we continue to pull this off? How can we keep up with the growing demand? What if the food runs out?* In that moment, the burden seemed too great to carry on my own. I suppose that was God's point. He didn't expect me to shoulder the weight alone.

I prayed, "God, how can I promise this many people food every single week?"

That's not your concern, Caroline, I felt God speak in my heart. *Just show up. I will provide.*

Fifteen years later, God continues to keep His promise. The food truck ministry reaches up to fifty thousand people a month, serving twenty-seven sites in different communities throughout the Los Angeles area five days a week. One million pounds of food flow through our food bank every month through all of the different feeding programs we have at the Dream Center. God has faithfully provided.

Make no mistake—I can't take any credit for how quickly

the food truck ministry came together. It was all God's doing! I was only responsible to be willing to walk on water. I had to show up, be on time, and be faithful during the process. I help coordinate things, but God is ultimately in charge. And it's only through His miraculous orchestration that any human effort can be multiplied and sustained, no matter what it is.

I've also noticed a personal side benefit: when I give my time to God, somehow I get more done in my personal life. It always seems that when I run errands on the days that I serve, parking lots are less crowded, I find everything in the store right away, and checkout lines are shorter, getting me home much sooner than expected. Call me crazy, but God does take care of the details!

The Bible says that when we pray in alignment with God's will, He will always provide what we need. "This is the confidence we have in approaching God: that if we ask anything according to his will, he hears us. And if we know that he hears us—whatever we ask—we know that we have what we asked of him" (1 John 5:14-15, NIV).

It's His will that we represent Him by healing the brokenhearted, reaching the lost, feeding the hungry, and clothing the homeless. So when we ask Him for anything in those areas that please Him, we can expect He will not only provide, but also multiply our efforts and give us more than enough. Trust me— or better yet, trust Him!—God will part seas, move mountains, and bring favor in unexpected places to accomplish what He has called you to do. As soon as you say yes to Him, opportunities to implement your trigger will appear, and you'll begin to make a difference, one life at a time.

CHAPTER 3

SERVING AND THE REALITIES OF LIFE

For everything there is a season.

ECCLESIASTES 3:1

I GROAN as the alarm sounds at 5:00 a.m. Thank goodness, I don't have to get up. The annoying bleep is rousing Matthew so he can catch a flight to some city to speak and raise money for the Dream Center. I try to go back to sleep, but he's making too much noise showering and packing for his trip. On his way out the bedroom door, Matthew kisses me on the forehead, and I groggily tell him, "Go get 'em, tiger." I toss and turn for a while and suddenly hear my wake-up call at 6:15. "Too soon," I mutter.

I shuffle down the hallway to wake up my daughter, Mia, repeating my attempts three to five times within fifteen minutes. I head to the kitchen to get the morning ritual started— make breakfast and pack her a lunch. I notice the time (yikes!) and try to hurry things along. By 7:00, Mia is sitting at the kitchen table gobbling her breakfast, and I'm double-checking that her homework is still in her backpack from last night's study session.

I can finally pour my first cup of coffee—in a thermal travel cup—to drink as I drive her to school. As Mia heads to the car, I run upstairs to wake up my son, Caden. I bundle him up in a blanket and run to the car where Mia waits. Half asleep, Caden mumbles, "I don't want to drop Mia off. I want to stay in bed."

Once Mia is dropped off at the Christian school, Caden and I head home. I feed him breakfast and get him ready for his first-grade homeschool class. By the time his teacher arrives at the house, it's time for my second cup of coffee and my time with God, studying the Word and praying. The quiet time is energizing and helps motivate me to start tackling the to-do list I make each night that relates to my roles as wife, mother, homemaker, friend, pastor, leader, and now author. From picking up dry cleaning to preparing a message for the upcoming weekend's women's conference to attending a PTA meeting— I'm ready to dive in. It's going to be a great but long day.

People often mistakenly believe that serving others will require an unmanageable sacrifice from them—personally, professionally, and emotionally. That hours spent at a homeless shelter will have negative effects on their own children left at home. Or that adopting a child may demand more of them than they can emotionally handle. Or that being a big sister to an inner-city kid may mean a person has to give up the thought of marriage.

Let me assure you that God does not call you to serve others at the expense of other areas of your life. Certainly there are seasons in our lives that make it difficult, even impossible, for us to do anything outside of managing our lives or our families. There are times our attention must be drawn toward taking care of important personal matters, like tending a sick child or dealing with a family crisis.

Our levels of willingness may change throughout our lives, but the key is staying consistent with what we can give and do.

Even now in my life there are times when I have more finances that I can give freely or more time to spend volunteering. And there are other times when I can't give or do as much. It's about being faithful in your particular season in life, not doing or giving out of guilt or with a begrudging attitude.

The fact is, I probably had more time and flexibility to serve others before I was blessed with my husband and, later, my two children. My life is so much richer with them. How Matthew and I ever got together in the first place is a miracle story of its own. Thankfully, God had plans to make it happen. Let me share my story before I unpack some balancing strategies for you.

The Relationship That Nearly Wasn't

I spoke to Matthew for the first time on my second visit to the church. As was customary at every service, he asked the congregation to turn to the person next to them and say hello. Imagine my surprise when twenty-two-year-old Matthew walked right off the stage and headed in my direction, where I sat in the second row on the end. Not only did he shake my hand and introduce himself, he asked if I would go on a date with him! I was taken aback, but flattered. "Sure," I beamed, with my shiny new braces. Within all of a few seconds, he told me to meet him at the Dream Center at six the following evening.

Then, as quickly as he popped up in front of me with his piercing blue eyes, he hopped back on stage to deliver his message. I didn't have time to process what had just happened until I drove home after the service. Because our encounter had been over in the blink of an eye, I wondered if I had imagined the whole thing. There was so much commotion that I doubted anyone around heard Matthew's request. I certainly didn't say a word to anyone about it.

The next day, I was a bundle of nerves. I hadn't moved to the Dream Center yet and was still working at Farmers Insurance. I was supposed to meet Matthew after work, so I took a little extra time in the morning getting ready. I knew I had found my calling at the Dream Center, but I didn't know if spending time with Matthew on a personal level was something God wanted me to do. So I went without expectations.

I waited for Matthew in the main parking lot at six o'clock. Ten minutes passed. No sign of him. *Maybe he got tied up with something*, I thought, rummaging through my car and cleaning it up a little. Twenty minutes. Still no Matthew. *Maybe he forgot?* After a half hour of staring down every car that entered the parking lot, wondering if it was him, I finally gave up. A youth service was starting at seven, so I slipped inside.

Truthfully, I was disappointed but also relieved. I felt God was protecting me from what probably would have been a dating disaster. I assumed Matthew's no-show was an obvious sign that he wasn't part of God's plan for me at the Dream Center.

Later that evening, the youth pastor, who had been waiting with Matthew, mentioned that they had been in another parking lot on the other side of the campus. Matthew and I couldn't have gotten in touch with each other since cell phones were still relatively uncommon and neither of us had one. I was bummed about the missed connection, but felt better that I hadn't been stood up. For the next two and a half years, although we saw each other around campus and had casual conversations about the ministries we were involved with, neither of us mentioned what had happened that night. I never said anything to Matthew because I figured if he was really interested in me, he would approach me again.

Random Encounters

A few months later, I was volunteering on a Saturday with a program called Adopt-A-Block, a door-to-door ministry where we assist people any way we can in a designated neighborhood. Most of the volunteers worked on this outreach every Saturday on different blocks. I had driven my vintage station wagon to the site. The car was hard to miss, especially with the trail of black exhaust it left in its wake.

At the end of the day, Matthew, who had been working on a nearby block, flagged me down. He needed a ride back to the Dream Center. *Oh no*, I groaned to myself. I was embarrassed to have him ride in my noisy clunker. If I could have managed it, I would have carried him on my back rather than have him go anywhere in my car. It was awkward, to say the least. Matthew and I practically shouted at each other the few minutes we were together, trying to hear what the other was saying over the obnoxious roar of the car's muffler. I was relieved when we finally parted ways.

Two and a half years after the first-date debacle, Matthew started calling me into his office for updates about the food truck ministry. After a while, I sensed that the meetings weren't really necessary; it was Matthew's excuse to see me. I definitely had a crush on him, but he was my pastor, so I didn't dwell on my growing feelings. I was confident God had someone special for me to share my life with. Even if it wasn't Matthew.

The Second First Date

Finally, for the second time, Matthew asked me out on a first date. We went to Disneyland with a delightful escort—his mom! She and I clicked from the start, especially since she had been born in Finland and adopted by Swedish parents. As we were walking along, she surprised me with a question in Swedish: "Would you marry my son?" Although my heart was pounding, I replied calmly and honestly in my native tongue, "I don't know, but I do like him." Poor Matthew didn't have a clue that we were talking about him.

But the question got me thinking about the qualities I admired in her son—Matthew's heart and love for people; his fearlessness, strength, and winning attitude that he maintained no matter how tough the situation; his contagious joy and kindness. At that moment I wasn't positive I wanted to be his wife, but I definitely knew I wanted to go out with him again.

On a Sunday afternoon soon after, we went horseback riding in Griffith Park. After we got something to eat, we went roller-skating for an hour or so. Halfway through our final lap, as I gazed into Matthew's eyes, some kids accidentally slammed into me. The next thing I knew I was outside, next to Matthew's car. Apparently after I fell, I had gotten up, finished skating, taken off my skates, and walked to the car with Matthew. Then I passed out. Someone inside the rink dialed 911.

When the paramedics arrived, Matthew was gently holding my head in his lap. They began asking me questions: "What's your name?" "How old are you?" "What year is it?" "Who is the president?" Then one of them asked, "Who is the man next to you?"

"The man of my dreams."

I don't remember saying those words, but Matthew definitely heard them. *She loves me!* It was the confirmation that he was waiting for.

That night I was supposed to manage an Easter Bunny photo booth at the mall, one way I raised money to support my ministry. When I got home from the hospital, I received news that our Easter Bunny had backed out. I needed to find a replacement within the hour. I couldn't do it; I was under doctor's orders to stay in bed for forty-eight hours. I was devastated that I might have to call the whole event off. Instead, for six long hours, the man of my dreams wore a hot, smelly bunny costume and posed with hundreds of kids.

That's when I knew he loved me.

But he wasn't ready to declare it quite yet.

The Surprise of a Lifetime

Two months later I got a letter from Bill Wilson, a friend of Matthew's in New York who started an organization called Metro Ministries and whom I had heard speak several times. Bill invited me to the Big Apple to help start their food bank and food truck ministries. I was thrilled. Bill's assistant, Cherry, picked me up at the airport and we drove into the city, chatting away like long-lost sisters. Because we would be extremely busy the entire week, Cherry said that if I wanted to do any sightseeing, today would be the best day. I agreed. The first stop? The Empire State Building.

On the observation deck, I squeezed in among all the other tourists to take in the breathtaking view of the New York skyline. Cherry directed my attention to the various landmarks. "There's the MetLife Building and there's the 59th Street Bridge." I nodded appreciatively.

As my eyes scanned the city, something diverted my attention on the deck, a few feet away. *Matthew?* He threw his arms around me and squeezed tight, then took my hand and pulled me out of the crowd.

Suddenly, he cupped his hands and shouted to the crowd. "Can I have everyone's attention?" My stomach fluttered and my hands were sweaty as he continued. "I want to let you all know that I love this woman more than any woman I could ever love in my life." When he dropped to one knee, there was a collective gasp.

"Caroline, will you marry me?" He pulled out a black box with a beautiful diamond ring inside.

I laughed and nodded, tears running down my face. The moment I had been waiting for was punctuated with thunderous applause.

A New Beginning

Three thousand people filled the parking lot of the Dream Center on September 10, 1999, to celebrate our wedding. The weather couldn't have been more perfect, and the sea of rented white chairs hid the potholes and grease stains on the asphalt. Matthew's father, Tommy, presided over the ceremony, and his closest pastor friends offered prayers and led Communion.

Enjoying the day with us were guests we bused from my remote food sites, the regulars from our homeless sites, pastors from across the country, and people from Matthew's home church in Arizona as well as our regular church members. The late Lou Rawls, who had been donating time and money to the Dream Center at that time, sang for us.

Afterward, the guests feasted on a potluck buffet as well as an elaborate six-foot-high wedding cake my mom made from a recipe in a French cooking magazine. Matthew and I never sat down or ate a morsel. We were too busy greeting and thanking people for sharing in our lives. It went on for the next four hours.

Steps to Stay Balanced

Today, two beautiful children later—Mia (nine) and Caden (six)—I continue to provide leadership at the Dream Center, dedicating my life to serving God, my family, and others. I wouldn't be completely honest if I didn't admit that there are challenging moments, especially when I feel there is not enough time to do all I need to do. Between juggling my family, my friends, and the countless responsibilities I have as a steward of service, it can be stressful.

And I can tell you that meshing a personal life with a life of service requires a balancing act that may take some time and effort, but it can be done. I often think of life as standing on top of a board balanced on a rolling barrel. If you want to maintain your balance, you have to constantly shift and adjust your position on the board.

Our priorities and needs change, depending on where we are in life and what our particular circumstances are. The key is to recognize that as seasons change, we need to reevaluate and refocus our attention on areas that may have been previously neglected.

Determine Priorities

The first step to staying balanced is to decide what is and is not a priority. Here's how I do it: I make a list of my responsibilities, goals, and tasks, and then I evaluate how much time I spend on them and what matters most. I remind myself of my mission in life—to be able to stand before God knowing that I fulfilled my call to love and be faithful to my husband, children, family, and friends—and determine my priorities based on this statement. Putting this step into practice has helped me learn how to live purposefully.

Eliminate Non-Priority Demands

Second, evaluate and eliminate the things in your life that don't contribute to what matters most to you. Cut out projects, demands, or requests that others may have persuaded you or pressured you to do. Stop taking tasks merely to please people. Avoid people who drain you or offer only negative energy. Keep your social networking interactions and television viewing to a minimum. Make fewer trips to the store. Make your time with friends worthwhile, not just a gossip fest.

For myself, I learned to cut back on my children's outside activities. I had made the mistake of overcommitting them to sports and other after-school activities because I wanted them to have a variety of experiences. My motives were good, but when I became involved to an unrealistic degree, it caused undue stress on our family as a whole and a lot of time mismanagement on my part. I've since limited my children's activities to what they are passionate about and what is realistic for the entire family.

Take Time for You

Third, find out what makes you a "better you" so that you can focus on and accomplish your priorities. Life can be tough. We all need to find an outlet to recharge our internal batteries and regain our strength. For some people, this means regular exercise, a hobby, reading, or attending a weekly get-together with uplifting friends. When you make time to do things you enjoy to unwind and recharge, you are better equipped to serve others in and outside of your family and to meet your priorities.

As an introvert, I recharge by spending time by myself. If I don't have regular alone time, I get cranky and overwhelmed. I have to set aside this "me time" in order to be at my best. Matthew is the exact opposite. A true extrovert, he regains his strength by being around crowds. Being alone drains and depresses him.

Keeping fit also helps clear and sharpen my mind and gives me lasting energy throughout the day. Six days a week, I pop in an exercise video or hop onto the elliptical machine for thirty minutes.

Of course, you can't spend more time doing these things than what you have prioritized. I love watching cooking shows because they relax me. I TiVo them so I can cut out the commercials. But I know there will be days when I have to turn off the television altogether because getting to bed earlier will make me more efficient at tackling the next day's priorities.

You Can Find a Balance

I understand that in today's world, balance is a commodity many of us believe we cannot afford. Women often feel pulled in every direction, stretched to the point of no return, running a hundred miles an hour, only to crash and burn at the end of the day. I don't believe God designed us to run ourselves ragged so that we begrudgingly serve Him. When God calls us to do something, He will equip us to get the job done.

I try to emulate the godly woman described in Proverbs 31. She is a woman of faith, of virtue, of integrity. She takes care of her family and her health. She is a wise steward of her time and finances. She is charitable and hardworking. The writer doesn't say that she served others at the expense of her own health, or that she took care of her family but ignored everything else. She had an appreciable amount of responsibilities and was able to balance them appropriately.

Mother Teresa had a good role model for learning the importance of love and sacrifice:

I'll never forget my own mother. She used to be very busy the whole day, but as soon as the evening came, she used to move very fast to get ready to meet my father. At that

time, we didn't understand, we used to smile, we used
to laugh, and we used to tease her. But now I remember
what a tremendous, delicate love she had for him. It didn't
matter what happened, she was ready there with a smile
to meet him. Today we have no time. The father and the
mother are so busy, the children come home and there's
no one to love them, to smile at them. That's why I'm very
strict with my co-workers. I always say: Family first. If you
are not there, how will your love grow for one another?[6]

God does not ask for your willingness to serve at the expense
of romancing your husband or wife, loving or spending time
with your children, pursuing your dreams or your career, or
sabotaging relationships with your friends. Making a difference
in the lives of others does take time, hard work, and sacrifice.
Most good things do. But it won't cost you the very things God
has blessed you with and wants you to have.

Stella Reed knows that's true. She serves with her husband,
Brad, in pastoring the New York Dream Center. With two kids
and a load of responsibilities to juggle, she has learned the art
of a balanced life. She shares:

I became a volunteer at the LA Dream Center right out
of high school. I was a bold, fearless, and crazy eighteen-
year-old ready to take on any challenge. I began to serve
in whatever capacity was needed. My heart for youth
began to grow immensely the more time I spent with
them. During the next twelve amazing years, I invested
in the lives of the young people. I also met and married
my best friend, Brad Reed, and we began our journey of
ministry together.

Three years ago, we began serving at the newly launched NYC Dream Center. It was heart-wrenching to leave LA, the youth, my friends, and everything I had ever known. But I knew I needed to be obedient to God's voice and He would handle the rest.

The change has stretched me and has forced me to grow. With two small children and another on the way, I have learned a few things about the importance of balance, priorities, and effectively working out my God-given calling. Here are a few things I have learned:

Stay connected to the Source: Everything flows from my relationship with Jesus. I have nothing to give to anyone if I am not daily surrendered to Him.

Determine your main priorities: I made a decision early on to make every moment in my life count, focusing on my main priorities.

Be present: I have learned the importance of being present wherever I am at the time. If I am home with my husband and kids, then I need to be fully engaged with them.

I truly believe there is nothing more impactful for the Kingdom than living out the daily joy of fulfilling our purpose in life. God has promised to give us everything we need to accomplish the purpose He has put us here to fulfill.

Serving Is a Privilege, Not a Burden

I often meet people who feel that helping others will drain them of energy and time and make them cranky, tired, and overwhelmed. They can't believe they can serve others without sacrificing every bit of themselves in the process.

Let me be clear. God intends for us to approach a life of service with joy. He doesn't want us to feel forced to serve others. He wants us to live with purpose, gladness, and a sense of adventure.

King Solomon, the wisest man who ever lived, said in Ecclesiastes 9:7-10,

> Seize life! Eat bread with gusto,
> Drink wine with a robust heart.
> Oh yes—God takes pleasure in *your* pleasure!
> Dress festively every morning.
> Don't skimp on colors and scarves.
> Relish life with the spouse you love
> Each and every day of your precarious life.
> Each day is God's gift. It's all you get in exchange
> For the hard work of staying alive.
> Make the most of each one!
> Whatever turns up, grab it and do it. And heartily!
> (*The Message*)

Did you notice how many exclamation points are in this passage? Talk about an enthusiastic pep talk! King Solomon encourages us to make the most of every day and live to the fullest. My friend Crystal lives a life of joy and adventure. Down through the years, serving others has not been burdensome for her; it's been a privilege.

Over twenty-four years ago, while serving as a
youth leader at a Youth Alive conference in Tacoma,
Washington, I had a life-changing moment.
    I had spent the day cleaning, washing floors, serving

lunch, encouraging, and praying for people. My heart was so full of joy. As I was thinking about all the people I had met and served that day, I heard the Lord whisper to my heart, *When you give, it shall be given back. You think this is just about giving money, but it's also about giving away your life. When you do it to the least of these, you do it unto Me.* His presence was so strong in that moment.

I knew God was calling me to leave all I knew. In the fall of 1995, I was watching a TV program and heard Pastors Tommy and Matthew Barnett [father and son] talking about the Dream Center. A year later, I became a part of the ministry.

Being in ministry is not so much what I do, but who I am. I have found no greater joy or privilege than giving all that has been given to me to all those the Lord brings along my path.

Serving others is more than something the Bible commands us to do. It is, in fact, a blessing that will not only change those around us, but will also make a difference in our own lives. Find your place, whatever season of life you're in, and help those in need. You'll never regret it.

CHAPTER 4

LOOK LONG ENOUGH

Learn to do good. Seek justice. Help the oppressed.
Defend the cause of orphans. Fight for the rights of widows.

--- ISAIAH 1:17 ---

ONE DAY IN 2006 I was having lunch with a woman who has a passion for orphans and children in foster care. As we munched on our salads, she shared information about orphans in the world, particularly in the United States, as well as foster children who get adopted. Then she said something that shocked me.

"Did you know that the majority of kids in California's foster-care system actually have loving and supportive parents?" I couldn't believe it. I assumed that every child was placed in foster care because parents had died, were addicted to drugs, physically or sexually abused their children, or simply abandoned them. Instead, the woman explained, these parents lost custody because, for whatever reason, they couldn't provide basic necessities such as food, clothes, a refrigerator, a stove, baby supplies, baby and toddler safety items, cribs, and beds. Sometimes even a home. What she shared tore me up inside.

Families in these situations are often reported to the local Department of Children and Family Services (DCFS) in California by a neighbor or teacher, someone who sees signs of neglect—frequent absences from school, unusual behavior or violent attitudes, obvious hygiene issues. DCFS investigates and compiles a list of requirements that must be fulfilled within a certain amount of time in order for parents to get their children back or to prevent them from being removed in the first place. Some lists are longer and harder to accomplish than others.

Over the next weeks, I began to research this for myself and learned that the situation has been going on for a long time.[7] In particular, as many as half of the 75,000 children in the Los Angeles County foster-care system "were needlessly placed in a system that is often more dangerous than the homes from which the children were taken."[8] I also had no idea that almost half a million children are in the foster-care system in the entire country.[9]

A Portrait of Brokenness

Imagine for a minute what it's like for parents who are doing their best to provide a safe and secure environment for their child. Maybe the sole provider for the household has left. Maybe a mother is battling a terminal disease and her savings are depleted, yet the medical bills keep coming. Maybe a father is working multiple jobs and still can't make ends meet. Imagine the desperation that permeates each of their lives.

Now imagine the anguish when a social worker knocks on their door to take their child away because at the end of the day their best isn't good enough. Imagine the overwhelming terror and inconsolable hurt of this mom or dad as they worry about the welfare of their child. Who is caring for my child? Where is he staying? Who is doing God-knows-what to her? Imagine this mom or dad, in tears and paralyzed by their dire straits within the system. Heartbreaking, isn't it?

Now picture a group of strangers knocking on their door and telling them they will provide whatever they need to keep or bring their child back home. Imagine the rush of gratitude. The abundance of joy. The flood of tears. Oh, the tears. This is a scene I've had the privilege of witnessing many times. It's a picture that makes my heart dance.

It's not wishful thinking to believe reuniting parents with their children is possible. It is possible if people are willing to walk on water and make it happen.

Getting out of the Boat

When Jesus told Peter to come and walk on water, Peter responded immediately. He didn't peek over the side of the boat, shake his head, and say, "Are you kidding me? No way!" He didn't question the impossibility of the situation. He didn't request a five-minute break to research how the laws of physics could be defied. He didn't turn to the other disciples and ask their opinions on whether or not he should step out. Peter followed Jesus. He trusted Him. He knew who his Master was. And without looking back, he stepped out into unknown waters.

I had to do the same thing.

Many people don't want to hear about the suffering in this world because they feel powerless to do anything about it. Others simply feel uncomfortable with the raw reality of injustice. They would rather pretend that iniquities like genocide, starvation, persecution, poverty, hunger, and homelessness don't exist or that they take place too far away to matter.

Here's some good news. You don't have to feel helpless, powerless, or uncomfortable. There is a solution. You can make a difference. You can effect change. If you're willing, God can use you to walk on water. If you're willing, He will equip you with

His power and resources so you can act as His person on the front lines to combat brokenness.

Trust me on this one—it's easier to submit to God and do what He asks of you than it is to avoid, ignore, or run away from Him. You never have to feel that you can't do or give enough. Don't look away from suffering. Look close and long.

Opening Your Eyes

Looking long enough means making a deep commitment to your trigger. Do your homework. Gain as much knowledge as you can. Research it online. Talk to people who have a similar passion and are making a difference. Glean insight from their experience.

Look—really look—at what you *can* do, whether it means feeding the hungry, mentoring a child, or organizing a day camp for inner-city kids. Don't just serve others or rally for a cause on a superficial level. Be a part of the experience. Get involved in the particulars of your trigger. Get to know those you help. Begin to understand their challenges, their needs, and their struggles. Dig deep and learn how they got where they are.

Robert, a former inner-city high school teacher, wanted to make a difference in the lives of teenagers. He had seen first-hand the young people trapped in destructive lifestyles and wanted to do what he could to be part of the solution. So he quit teaching and went into full-time ministry with troubled youth. Here is how Robert looked long enough:

> I grew up with great parents who loved me and sacri-
> ficed to give me the best possible shot at a successful life.
> Though they supported me fully in my endeavors, I can't
> say they were excited about my decision to become a
> high school teacher in the inner city of Los Angeles.

As I began to work with teenagers, I quickly realized that many of them needed more help than just a youth service at an inner-city church. If they didn't get out of their communities, a sense of hopelessness was a very real probability for most of them; jail and even death were good possibilities for others.

When one of my students, a high school soccer player, was gunned down in the street, it reinforced my thinking. The young man's picture in my office is a reminder of why I do what I do.

I had to leave full-time teaching. God had moved my heart and He was inviting me back into full-time ministry through the Dream Center, which provides a residential home for teens in trouble, teens who want to start over.

Today, I run the residential program, a private school, and the youth ministry at the Dream Center as well as minister weekly in the Central Juvenile Hall here in Los Angeles. I've seen lives changed forever and I've seen lives lost. It still breaks my heart to see young men in juvenile detention who are headed for a life in prison or death. Every day I ask myself, *What more can we do to reach them?*

God's Plan Takes Shape

I couldn't stop thinking about the lunch conversation about orphans and foster-care children I had had with my friend. The wheels started turning in my mind. *If "stuff," albeit essential things, is all that's needed to keep a family together, I can find a way to make that happen. By mobilizing our efforts and resources at the Dream Center, we can provide what is needed to create safe and healthy family environments and prevent families from being split up in the first place.*

Within a month, the women of our church and I launched Project Prevention, a foster-care intervention program designed to keep children with their families. Though the first year we faced some challenges finding the right leadership to head the program, we worked through the setbacks and remedied some of our mistakes, and eventually established effective ways to maximize our efforts.

We had a great head start with the Dream Center's resources at our disposal—a sizable inventory of donated clothes, cleaning products, baby supplies, and furniture from individuals and corporations. Then we packed up groceries from our food bank, grateful for the provisions we could contribute to stabilize families and help them stay together.

James is one of the many single parents we've helped over the years. James is a hard worker, but he barely makes enough for rent and struggles to provide food for his daughter, so we have partnered with him. Every Friday afternoon, James picks up a week's worth of groceries.

Do you see a need for a similar program in your community, whether it involves providing food or other tangible goods? It doesn't have to be as large as the Dream Center's program. It can start with meeting one need. As you willingly step out, God will direct you to the right people with the right hearts in your community and among your friends and family to build a stockpile of necessities for any need.

Danielle is a wife and mother of two. Every two to three weeks, she pulls into our parking lot with her SUV packed from top to bottom with diapers, clothes, and other house supplies for Project Prevention.

Whenever she learns about a specific item that's needed, Danielle e-mails her friends and posts a request on Facebook asking for donations. She schedules pickups and then delivers what she has collected to the church. Danielle's networked donors contribute regularly, each person feeling privileged to be called upon.

Partnering with Others

When we first came up with the idea for Project Prevention and stepped out in faith, we didn't have a clue what sort of influence we could have on these families or if there were any legal parameters. We also weren't sure whether the state's social workers would allow us to intervene or whether they even wanted us to help in the first place. Would they be suspicious or prejudiced against us, thinking we had an ulterior motive because we were a religious organization?

We contacted the local DCFS chapter and let them know what we could provide. We didn't have a formal strategy to partner with the government, just a strong desire to serve the local social services agency. We wrote and submitted a plan of what we dreamed Project Prevention would look like and began to outline what we could offer. Then we hounded the local DCFS office until someone was willing to take a chance on us.

The social workers did question our commitment as we were ironing out the initial kinks in our program. They were accustomed to people who seem willing to help, but never follow through with their promises. Before long we proved how willing and able we were to step in and make ourselves available to them. After we successfully helped a few families, word spread like wildfire. DCFS started referring us on a regular basis to families in need. We went from making a difference in one family's life to serving fifteen families in just a few short weeks. Today, we are contacted with new referrals three or four times a day.

In our case, what we may have lacked in experience was made up for with our consistency and commitment. I believe that was the key that solidified a long-term relationship.

While having a plan is important to pursue your trigger, it's equally important to have a willing and committed heart. If you are trying to link efforts with others to relieve a need—whether it's with a governmental department, a corporation, or even another volunteer organization—you must act on your willingness. You must be so committed that others know they can count on you. You have to be faithful. You have to consistently show up. You have to be available. You have to do the work and get the job done right. This is how you build lasting partnerships.

I am thankful that the United States has social service agencies on the federal and local levels, both of them striving to assist in maintaining a livable standard for all people. We do not work against the system or assume we can do a better job. We work with them for the sake of the children and families who need help.

Making a Local School Better

We at the Dream Center often team up with others for the greater good. In our part of Los Angeles, schools have often been ranked low academically. So two years ago we decided to explore the question of whether there was anything we could do. Matthew set up a meeting with the principal and teachers at Rosemont Elementary School nearby.

"I want all of you to know how thankful we are for you," Matthew began. "It's obvious that you love your students and the members of our community, but we know you are hindered by small budgets and no resources. You are fighting an uphill battle and we want to help." The school officials, who had received only complaints and criticism before, couldn't believe what Matthew was saying and openly wept.

Since our partnership began, we have updated their computer lab, supplied volunteer help, read to and tutored the kids, donated school supplies, offered incentive programs (like donating bikes and electronic devices to the kids who consistently get good grades and high marks for good behavior), and given them food and clothing.

A combination of willingness, cooperation, and a cohesive team spirit has created a match made in heaven. Recently one of the elementary school's staff members expressed his gratitude in an e-mail:

Thank you for sending us volunteers during the first week of school. The volunteers were a tremendous help with delivering books to the classrooms, organizing the resource room, and sweeping the school grounds. All of these tasks would have taken days and/or weeks to complete! We are immensely grateful for your continued support of our students, teachers, and school. . . . We are thankful that the Dream Center has become one of Rosemont's most generous community partners. Because of the stressful climate of education, the economy, and family life, we realize the need to seek monetary, service, and volunteer support from the various organizations in our community. We cannot do it alone! We look forward to continue working with our community partners such as you to enhance our students' academic needs, motivation, and emotional health.

So look long enough to discover how you can couple with others to fill needs within your community. Be proactive. Take the initiative and make the first move if others don't reach out for help. Contact your local school board, volunteer organizations, government program, YMCA outreaches, and even other churches. Collectively you can make a difference.

What We Do

Our first step at Project Prevention is to conduct an initial visit with the family's social worker to determine whether we are the right fit for the family and how we can help. We make our assessments and schedule a delivery. If the family is in need of ongoing assistance like food, toiletries, or diapers, we add them to our weekly route of deliveries for six months. After that time, we reassess their situation and determine whether they are able to function without assistance or estimate how much more time they need to close their case with the state.

We provide much more than tangible items. We teach the families how to be frugal and practical. For instance, we show them how they can use just enough soap (whether bar soap or dishwashing liquid) so it doesn't need to be replenished as often. In addition, much of our ministry focuses on spiritual and emotional support. We offer counseling. We provide transportation to church, pray with them, and even hold Bible studies in their homes if they're willing. We encourage them to dream again and reinforce that we care and understand their struggles. We also extend temporary housing to some of the families, those who would never be able to get back on their feet without having a place to stay. While these parents receive an education or learn a job skill or trade, they stay on our family floor until they are ready to move out on their own.

You can do the same thing on a smaller scale in your community. Talk to your family, friends, people at church, or neighbors about individuals or families who are going through a rough time and need help. You may learn about a single mom, a person who recently lost his or her spouse, parents of a terminally ill child, a family whose home has burned down, or an adult battling cancer. There is always something you can do to fill a need. Donate clothes. Clean someone's house. Bring dinner on a regular basis. Make school lunches. Buy groceries. Put together a gift basket of baby supplies.

Look long enough, find a need, and fill it.

Helping Lucia

One of the women that Project Prevention helped was Lucia, a mother who was on the verge of losing her four children (ages five, eight, ten, and sixteen) to the state. Her husband, the father of all four kids, had been deported. The family lived in a dangerous housing project notorious for gang activity. The mother's two older boys were constantly getting in trouble at school—when they showed up, which they rarely did. Their frequent absences had prompted the school to report the mother to DCFS. I think the boys' rebellion stemmed from their father's absence and they were looking for love and acceptance on the streets.

After the initial visit, Becky and Kelly, volunteers on our team, arrived at the house with food, furniture, and hygiene and cleaning products. Becky will never forget that memorable day.

> We were very excited to be able to help Lucia and her family. But the look on her face when she came out of her house was very disheartening and confusing. She was

terrified and ran over to the truck, begging us not to take her children away from her.

When we tried to open the back of the truck to get the supplies, she fell against the doors, trying to close them. Both Kelly and I tried to comfort her and explain who we were and why we were there. When she finally allowed us to open the doors of the truck and she saw all the supplies we were giving her family, she fell to her knees and cried out of her gratitude. Then she ran inside the house and grabbed her children to help us unload the truck. They were excited too.

Lucia and her family will always have a special place in my heart, helping me to remember the importance of loving and serving families who need someone to believe in them.

This woman was able to keep her kids, and her file was closed. Though she attends church regularly, her boys still struggle. I'm hopeful it won't be long before they, too, experience a life change.

Sometimes I wonder why we spend so many hours each week within our church's four walls when it's so much more thrilling to use our faith to be heroes on behalf of God in the world. I'm not telling you to stop going to church or that it's not important. I'm just suggesting we need to broaden our focus and invest our time outside the comforts of our familiar spiritual territory.

Each year since Project Prevention's inception, our team has been able to save about two hundred families from being split apart (our goal is to increase the number to four hundred a year). We've also witnessed the wonderful moments when fifty families were reunited.

Discerning Where Brokenness Begins

Over the years, those of us involved in this outreach have detected root issues that we believe have contributed to the brokenness of the individuals involved. When families arrive at the Dream Center, they receive counseling, are tested for their education level, and are assessed for their natural gifts and talents. This information helps us better equip and guide them into the workplace.

When you start meeting a need, you usually uncover more needs beneath the surface, some of which are root problems. It's a natural progression of looking long enough. The number one issue we have found is the impact of the individuals' environment. The situation people are in when they arrive tends to be remarkably similar to what they experienced as a child or teenager.

The people who are part of Project Prevention have no idea what a better life even looks like, let alone how to achieve it. Most of them come from abusive homes, then marry or have relationships with abusive people. They don't have a biblically stable and healthy foundation to equip them to be self-sufficient and emotionally whole, and to live with purpose and meaning. Most of them have not had any encouragement or positive reinforcement from mentors or loved ones. So they continue to experience the vicious cycle of what is familiar to them—an unhealthy environment and lifestyle.

Emotionally, they've built walls around their hearts to protect themselves from being disappointed or feeling unloved. Sadly, when these walls begin to crumble and their vulnerability is exposed, many of them quit the program. The process scares them. They'd rather hide behind their walls because it makes them feel safer and more comfortable. Unfortunately, nothing will change for the better if they don't let down their guard and allow God to work. It breaks my heart when I hear about those who have decided to return to their old ways.

For those participants who stay in the program and commit to inner healing, most experience a change in their emotional health and mental outlook. Kelli, our program director, surveyed families who had been at the Dream Center for more than a year, comparing their responses to the ones they'd given to the same questions when they arrived. Here is what she found:

- 63 percent (versus 7.6 percent upon entering the program) felt that others accepted them unconditionally
- 72 percent (versus 30 percent) felt that they have people in their lives who make them feel safe
- 63 percent (versus 30 percent) felt that they have people in their lives whom they can ask for help
- 81 percent (versus 23 percent) felt loved

I am inspired and encouraged to see this kind of inner transformation. I know once we tackle these root problems, there is hope for a total life change.

Why Education Matters

What I've discovered with the families involved with Project Prevention is how many of the parents lack basic education skills. In fact, a majority test at first, second, and third grade levels. One particular mom in her forties, who had six children (two of whom were grown and no longer lived at home), couldn't even read. I had no idea how this woman had gotten as far as she had in life. I was impressed by her survival skills.

We sent her to tutoring classes off campus. As with all of our programs, we try not to reinvent the wheel if a particular need is already being met by established organizations nearby. Though we do offer GED classes and professional counseling to service the needs of our in-house residents, we outsource some of the other participants' individual needs.

I sympathized with this woman. She would come back to the Dream Center frustrated and embarrassed because she was the oldest woman in the literacy class and had a hard time keeping up with the other students. Finally one day, she broke down and told me her story. This woman had been molested by her father as a little girl and, as a result, placed in foster care. She was bounced around to more than thirty homes until she was emancipated at the age of eighteen.

This woman had to fend for herself without money, family support, education, or any job skills. The truth is, she is a survivor and has done the best she could do. It makes me sad that no one in her entire life loved her enough to teach her a basic skill like reading, something that most of us take for granted. Now this woman has the opportunity to learn to read because someone was willing to walk on water and teach her.

It's Our Job to Step Out

I was doing some reading on illiteracy in America and found the following statistics:

> 45 million adults in the United States are marginally illiterate.[10]
> More than three out of four people on welfare can't read.[11]
> According to the United Way, illiteracy costs businesses and taxpayers $20 billion a year.[12]

What shocked me most was reading that "to determine how many prison beds will be needed in future years, some states actually base part of their projection on how well current elementary students are performing on reading tests."[13]

We are actually planning for people to fail instead of planning how to prevent them from failing. Some might argue that it's the government's job to educate our kids. Isn't that why we send them to school every day? But that doesn't sit well with me. I find it hard to believe that American adults cannot read because their state's educational system failed them. I don't think it's that simple.

When this fortysomething mom first walked into our facility, she looked like a little lost girl. In the three years she was with us, she made tremendous strides. She left our facility testing at a fifth-grade level, which makes her eligible to pursue her GED. Her children have also benefited spiritually, emotionally, and educationally. They caught up with their class levels and received a strong foundation of faith and love. Each member of this family has been given a glimpse that life can be different. Though they are no longer with us, I pray they will use the tools they learned at the Dream Center to continue to grow in their understanding of God and pursue their education.

Life after Foster Care

I have found another common denominator among the parents living on the family floor as well as among the many residents who have stayed at the Dream Center throughout the years. Many of them have spent time in the foster-care system. This fact prompted me to research what happens when a child is emancipated.

Please hear my heart. I'm aware of and appreciate the

countless foster parents who do a wonderful job of loving, providing for, and taking care of their foster children. I've met many of them. I admire and respect these parents for raising foster children as their own and giving them an education and skills so they can thrive in life once they legally become adults. Sadly, many foster kids aren't so lucky to have loving foster parents who care enough to invest in their lives.

Once foster children turn eighteen, they are legally on their own. For a large number of foster parents, there's not much incentive to allow these almost-adults to stay in the home, especially since the monthly government checks to help support the child end. Many of these children sever ties with the foster parents and the social worker. They embark on their new life lacking a good education, life and job skills, and the resources it takes to create a successful life. Many of them also suffer emotional scars from their past, having been sexually abused, abandoned, or rejected.

In 2010, Human Rights Watch published a report titled "My So-Called Emancipation" that details the struggles of young people who leave foster care. The publication suggests that around 20 percent of the approximately 20,000 youth leaving foster care in California each year will become homeless. Of the young adults interviewed, the majority lacked basic living skills; they had no plan for housing, no means of supporting themselves, and essentially nowhere to go.[14]

One of the men in our discipleship program shared what it was like being bounced around different foster homes as a child and what his life was like after he was emancipated. His story gives a good idea of how difficult it is for teenagers to transition to life on their own. Reading about his experience underscores why it's so important to minister to children who are struggling in the system: so they can live a better life when they leave their foster homes. Our friend shares,

> My first memories were of being in foster care between the ages of three and five years old. I was moved around to several different foster homes because my mother was trying to kidnap my eight siblings and me. My first memory of being molested was when I was seven years old. It was a friend of my foster parents who told me that if I said anything, I would be killed and so would my siblings. The abuse continued for three years until I was moved to another foster home. There I experienced more abuse and molestation.
>
> I was moved back and forth between institutional boys' homes and foster homes. I was bullied, taunted, beaten, and sexually abused, often by friends and relatives of those who were responsible for my well-being. Eventually I found myself in several juvenile detention centers around the LA area until I was finally emancipated at the age of seventeen.
>
> When I left the foster-care system, I was a broken young man. I despised any kind of authority and trusted no one. I struggled to have healthy relationships. I was homeless several times, turned to drugs, and got involved in criminal activity, eventually ending up in jail. I was living a hopeless life, not knowing where I was going to end up or if there was anything left for me to live for.

It's easier to stop the bleeding of a scrape or gash than of a gaping wound. As we've worked with Project Prevention families, we've come to realize that it would have been so much easier to help these teenagers as soon as they were emancipated, before they started having children of their own.

Our women's ministry is in the process of tackling this injustice by helping to support emancipated foster kids. We are currently planning to open a home for about a hundred young adults to give them the best possible chance at becoming successful in life. When I started writing this book, we had raised only 50 percent of our goal, but I had faith God would provide. By the time I was finished, God had provided every penny. Plans are finally underway to open that home.

The Effects of Living in the System

There are many reasons why a child ends up in foster care. Studies show that children in the system who jump from their birth parents' home to multiple foster homes experience long-term, damaging consequences. On average, children are moved to three different foster homes,[15] though it's not unheard of for some to be bounced around to twenty, even thirty different homes.[16] Of course, the longer children stay in the foster-care system until they age out, the more foster homes they will live in. Obviously, this creates a lack of stability and consistency that children need in order to thrive in life.

The American Academy of Pediatrics warns that "the emotional consequences of multiple placements or disruptions are likely to be harmful at any age. . . . Multiple moves while in foster care (with the attendant disruption and uncertainty) can be deleterious to the young child's brain growth, mental development, and psychological adjustment."[17]

When I read "My So-Called Emancipation" report from the Human Rights Watch, I was in tears. Reading the stories of those who were in and out of foster homes was heartbreaking.

Phillip, one of the young people interviewed, had been in foster care since he was seven years old. "I can't even count how many [foster] homes or placements I was in. I think it was between 20 and 25. Age seven to 13 was really rough."[18] For kids like Phillip, it's nearly impossible to make connections, form relationships, and build friendships when you're constantly moving around. Without these important social connections, it's difficult to build a healthy, productive, and successful life as a child and then again as an adult.

But that's not all.

The National Center for Youth Law reported that around 25 percent of former foster kids have been arrested and spent time incarcerated. About 33 percent receive public assistance. Also, the unemployment rate among former foster children is more than 50 percent.[19] Then we have the high financial price exacted by foster care. United Friends of the Children, an organization dedicated to advocating for children in foster care, estimates the direct cost of foster care nationally at $33 billion, or $80,000 per child. Foster care in California alone costs about $4.7 billion annually, with the highest number of foster kids in the country, 100,000.[20]

These statistics aren't merely numbers representing the astronomical amount of money we spend on children shuffled into foster care. They represent the natural progression of the consequences these kids ultimately experience. Did you know about 70 percent of prisoners and 80 percent of death row inmates were former foster kids?[21]

We are the product of what has been poured into us. What if members of the body of Christ who have a trigger to help children in foster care adopted or mentored a child? Can you imagine what would happen if they used their willingness to love on and believe in these kids, to give them a real chance at life? In a few years, I'm confident we would see these numbers decline.

What Love and Willingness Can Do

When I think about the power of a willing heart embracing the foster-care system, I think about Ida. She has experienced a better life because two people stepped out to walk on water and adopt her.

I was a biracial baby, born out of wedlock, who was adopted as a newborn by white parents at the end of the civil rights movement. I am thankful to my biological mother for not aborting me. The pressure she felt from her own family must have been intense. I am reminded of her when I read Proverbs 23:25, "May she who gave you birth be happy." I hope that she is.

My adoptive parents, Olga and Ilmar, were willing to take a chance on me. Mom, who was Estonian, had experienced racism and prejudice firsthand. When Hitler and Stalin "split" Europe, she and her niece were on one of the last trains out of Estonia. She never saw her parents or her brother again. She met my father, a Finnish-American, in Germany where he was stationed with the army. They were married and returned to the States.

Mom went to great lengths to make sure that I "fit in" wherever we lived. She wanted to make sure that I didn't stand out or feel different because I was adopted or because of my race. These issues were never discussed in my house, but they were issues that I would face on my own later.

I've had a great life (including a full basketball scholarship to Loyola Marymount University) because of the love and support of my parents. Today I work for the Dream Center. Many of the people we serve are in their situations because of abuse and poor parenting, while others had a Christian upbringing but chose to go their own way. Sometimes the only difference in my story and theirs is the fact that I had stable, hardworking, and loving parents who were proud of me.

I identify with the story of Jesus feeding the five thousand. The crowd's number was based only on the men being counted, not the women and children who were there. And yet the huge crowd was fed from a little boy's lunch, a boy who had not even been counted. God uses people that other people don't count. That's what my parents did for me and what the Dream Center does every day for others.

Making Changes One Step at a Time

I know that the problems of the foster-care system cannot be solved overnight and that these are not the only problems facing our society today. But I truly believe that positive world changes begin with children. And I know from firsthand experience that it is possible to do something about it, step by step, one child at a time.

We can stop the bleeding. We can save our country billions of dollars annually. But even more valuable than the dollars saved is saving a generation from foster care, correctional facilities, and welfare. We can stop the vicious cycle of generation after generation of people who grow up without love, not knowing how to live productive, purposeful lives. Foster kids are God's children, and they are meant to accomplish their dreams and enjoy their lives.

Sometimes we act as if we're weak, as if we are powerless, as if we're helpless. We simply don't think we can make a difference. There are 246,780,000 soldiers in the Christian army in the United States alone.[22] More than 250,000 children enter the foster-care system every year, and today there are 104,000 children in foster care waiting to be adopted.[23] Only .04 percent of Christians would need to adopt to take care of every child in the system. We can eliminate this problem. We can be the answer. We are strong and powerful in Christ.

The Difference We Can Make

When we first opened up the family floor in the Dream Center to the Project Prevention families, we asked DCFS how much money we were saving them. One of the supervisors did some calculations based on a family of nine who were part of our program and told us that "savings to DCFS would be $453,600 for the 2010 year."[24]

By helping just seven children, we were able to save the state of California and taxpayers $453,600! Imagine what we, as the body of Christ, can do throughout the country with our entire army. Imagine how many children and how much money that adds up to.

Safe Families for Children (SFFC), an organization based in Chicago, is making a huge impact in the lives of foster children. When parents find themselves in a crisis and are temporarily unable to provide for their children, Christian families open their homes to these children in the interim. As the parents look for jobs, find a place to live, or do whatever needs to be done to create a secure home environment, their children are cared for by willing and loving families. SFFC is making enough of a difference in Chicago that some social services agencies consider the group dangerous because the organization is putting their jobs on the line. But that hasn't stopped the church member–supplied network from expanding to more than thirteen states and still counting.[25]

This is what happens when believers are willing to walk on water.

Perhaps there is an area of injustice you have avoided or ignored because it hurts too much to face. Guess what? It just might be the cause God wants you to champion. Look long enough to hurt. Be willing. You'll be surprised what can happen when you take action and partner with God. You might help solve problems that others consider unfixable. Don't be a bystander while those around you suffer. Use your influence and initiate change where you see a need.

CHAPTER 5

WALK WITH CONFIDENCE

---

*You have already won a victory . . . because the Spirit who lives
in you is greater than the spirit who lives in the world.*

— I JOHN 4:4 —

PETER STARTED OUT his miraculous walk on water with confidence. "Tell me if it's really you, Lord, and I'll do it. I'll come
to you" (Matthew 14:28, my paraphrase). The man had total
faith in Jesus. Though some would say this bullheaded disciple
had a knack for putting his foot in his mouth, in this instance
Peter showed willingness. He believed if Jesus was involved, he
could step out and walk on the shimmery surface of the lake as
if it were solid ground.

Did Peter have the skills to walk on water? No. Did he have
the ability in his own strength to walk on water? No. The only
thing he had that was required of him was a willingness to
step out in faith. Willingness, coupled with confidence in God,
brings about exciting, life-changing results.

But sometimes we become overconfident with our own
abilities and forget about God. We begin to boast that it is our
gifts, talents, smarts, beauty, or brawn that makes things happen. Some might think a person's Ivy League education will

guarantee he or she can build a successful not-for-profit organization or committee. Or that natural leadership skills and charm are what will win over a team of volunteers to run a soup kitchen.

Certainly, God will use our gifts and talents to do what He has called us to do, but we can't rest on our laurels. We must be confident in what He can do through us, not what we can do for Him. The moment we take our eyes off Him is the moment we will start to feel the waves lapping around our ankles and pulling us down into the deep.

Taking a leap—or even a step—of faith may feel uncomfortable or even terrifying at first, but you can confidently continue on your journey, knowing God is on your side. The apostle Paul knew that confidence and encouraged other believers (including us today), "Now all glory to God, who is able, through his mighty power at work within us, to accomplish infinitely more than we might ask or think" (Ephesians 3:20).

No Limits with God

I am blessed to see God constantly at work in the lives of others, doing the impossible. The story that touches my heart the most is Tommy Hollenstein's. His life dramatically changed on March 10, 1985, when he broke his neck in a biking accident. Tommy could feel himself leaving his body and begged God for another chance at life. When he regained consciousness, he was paralyzed from the neck down, and he is now confined to a wheelchair.

Tommy spent the next six months in rehab. There his therapists tried to teach him to paint using his mouth, but he felt it was too restrictive.

Tommy came to the Dream Center in 1993 and was immediately struck by the heartfelt ministry we had established for physically challenged individuals. He started attending church regularly and developed a personal relationship with the Lord. Twelve years after his first painting class in rehab, God inspired Tommy to do a collaborative painting with his first service dog, Weaver. Tommy applied different colors of wet paint to an over-sized canvas and rolled through the paint in his wheelchair, creating beautiful abstract designs. Then Weaver added his own paw-print touches to Tommy's painting.

Since then, Tommy has continued to make his amazing art pieces. He has shown his work in New York, Boston, Los Angeles, and London, winning many competitions along the way. He has steadily been selling his artwork and every year donates an original piece to the Dream Center to be auctioned off at one of the major fund-raising events.

I get so excited when I think of what God can do when we partner with Him. I've learned that anything is possible. There are no limits.

The Dream Center's Partnership with God

I love talking about the Dream Center and the miracles that keep us operating. Our story speaks of God's faithfulness and His continuous provision. When you look at some of the obstacles we've faced on our journey and the mind-boggling financial cost of running the organization, one thing is clear—God is involved. Otherwise, none of our success makes sense. If we looked only to our human strength, efforts, and abilities, we would never have been able to accomplish all that we do or have all the resources to facilitate healing.

Frankly, it's a wonder my husband can sleep at night, let alone sleep soundly (which he does!). His constant challenges including figuring out how to come up with half a million dollars every month to operate the Dream Center; finding long-term volunteers and leaders to help run our two hundred programs; and maintaining a sense of security, knowing that some of the broken people we help have questionable and even criminal pasts.

Every day the Dream Center has existed has been a miracle, made possible by a team of tireless individuals. It demands living right, staying focused, and never giving up. It warrants countless hours of planning, researching, organizing, brainstorming, and creating. But it all began with a willingness to walk on water.

God's Vision

Matthew came to Los Angeles with a lofty dream: to establish and pastor a megachurch like his father, Tommy Barnett, had done in Phoenix, Arizona. But the dream eluded him. One night Matthew was walking in Echo Park when God opened his eyes to the brokenness of the city. Matthew saw people who needed help. People who were afraid, in trouble, sick, poor, homeless, and hungry.

It was clear that God wanted Matthew to shift his energies to help others. He started the Dream Center in 1994 to bring the gospel to the lost and heal the hurting. It wasn't a conventional church; it was a twenty-four-hour "hospital" to meet the spiritual, mental, emotional, and physical needs of others.

In this area, a mile away from downtown Los Angeles, Matthew started going door to door in the neighborhood, meeting people and asking if they needed anything. Many times he would buy groceries for people with money from his own pocket. He learned Spanish so he could better communicate with his neighbors.

One day, Matthew got the attention of some of the local

gang members when he set up some weights and gym equipment in an empty lot next to the church. He invited them to work out and soon they joined him, bragging that they were bulking up in preparation for prison.

Within two years, the outside gym ministry flourished. As I've said before, helping in one area uncovers other areas that need work. As more outreach programs were created to meet the needs of the community, the Dream Center outgrew its facilities. Matthew's vision expanded. He was driving down the freeway one day and noticed the vacant Queen of Angels Hospital, which had closed its doors in 1986. As soon as his eyes fell on the massive building, he envisioned each of its fifteen floors being used to help a different social need in the community.

Big Dreams, Big Faith

Matthew did some investigating and found out the Catholic church owned the property. They were seeking to sell it for $25 million, and an offer was already on the table from Paramount Studios for $15 million. Tommy and Matthew shared their dream of a spiritual hospital with the nuns, but also admitted they couldn't match $15 million. They made an offer of $3.9 million, not mentioning they actually only had $30,000 in the bank.

The nuns accepted their bid with one stipulation—the mortgage had to be paid off within eighteen months. The pressure was on. Matthew and Tommy morphed into fund-raising roadrunners. For the next year and a half, they made phone calls, they traveled, and they talked to anyone who could help. At the eleventh hour, which seems to be God's favorite time, the last $2 million came through. The deadline was only a few days away.

God does work in unusual ways. The man who donated a

million dollars and then convinced his son to donate the last million actually thought Matthew's vision was a joke, a waste of time. As a matter of fact, this man told my father-in-law the best hope for Los Angeles was to drop a bomb on the city and start over. And yet, he was still moved to help. When he saw the Dream Center in action, his mind and heart changed. He, too, was willing to walk on water through his financial gift.

It seemed impossible to find a facility perfectly suited for their needs. Matthew and Tommy walked on water. It seemed impossible to purchase a $25-million property with an offer ridiculously below the asking price. They walked on water. It seemed impossible to get a mortgage of $3.9 million and pay it off in a year and a half. They walked on water. When God puts something on your heart to do and you follow willingly, you can walk on water, even when everything seems impossible.

Last year, the Dream Center was appraised at $56 million. God knew what He was doing when the nuns insisted that the mortgage be paid off in eighteen months. With operational costs running between $500,000 and $600,000 every month, Matthew and Tommy could never have afforded a mortgage on top of those expenses. Not only that, but after they purchased the hospital, they had to invest millions of dollars to renovate the aging building. And the church was growing so fast that they needed a bigger auditorium.

It seemed as soon as they turned the corner on one miracle, another development required immediate divine intervention. There was never a dull moment or a time they could put up their feet and enjoy a well-deserved break. *Break?* I don't think Matthew or Tommy know the meaning of the word.

In 1998, plans were drawn up and costs researched for con-

structing a bigger church on the bus parking lot. The ballpark
figure given was $2.5 million. With that information, we spent
the next few years raising money and searching possible new
locations, such as nearby vacant concert halls as well as the shut-
tered Palladium theater in Hollywood.

A New Direction

Sunday after Sunday, our church of six hundred people squeezed
into an old basketball gym for services. We packed as many
folding chairs into the tight space as was physically possible.
When we sat down, our knees were pressed into the chair in
front of us. People crammed onto the stage, sitting Indian style,
when room on the gymnasium floor ran out. We didn't have air-
conditioning, so the summer months were almost unbearable.
Yet God displayed His love and power there.

In 2001, Matthew and Tommy got a phone call from a
leader in the Foursquare Church. Their headquarters and his-
toric church, Angelus Temple, was within walking distance of
the Dream Center. The church had been one of our faithful
partners in replenishing our food bank.

The church was undergoing internal changes, and Matthew
and I were offered its leadership. We accepted the challenge and
Matthew became senior pastor. Tommy flew from Phoenix to
Los Angeles once a week to help run the fund-raising programs
at the Dream Center.

Angelus Temple seats three thousand people and was valued
in excess of $30 million ten years ago. The congregation was in
the midst of a massive $8 million church renovation project.
Matthew and his father were able to offer input into the design.
And the final drawback to the property—no accommodations

for parking—was remedied a while later with a new seven-story parking deck.

The Temptation to Give Up

The Dream Center was growing by leaps and bounds. We were finally able to expand to two Sunday services with enough room for all. But there was still a lot of work to be done on the property. The nine buildings we owned from our initial purchase were being used to capacity and from the start needed some work. By 2008, it was time to launch a massive renovation project. In particular, ten floors of the hospital needed to be completely gutted, brought up to code, and repaired after earthquake damage. The cost? Thirty-six million dollars. We couldn't believe it. There was no way we could possibly afford it.

The beloved Dream Center felt like a money pit. We had already poured millions of dollars into it—every dollar costing us blood, sweat, and tears to obtain. It was the first time I had seen Matthew discouraged.

For fourteen years Matthew had grasped at straws, trying to make ends meet and trusting God the miracles would keep on coming. But this time was different. The dollar amount we needed to reach the finish line felt like a crushing blow. Even though we thought we were so close, our dream felt so far away. When Matthew heard how much the renovations would cost, he couldn't hide his discouragement.

He received the news in New York City. Two weeks earlier, we had started a Dream Center in New York, and Matthew was traveling to the East Coast every week to help with the project. He was exhausted. Here's how Matthew reacted at the time:

My thought when I heard the figure—$36 million— was simple: *this project is over.* The leap of faith we took to purchase the hospital was a mistake. All the hard work, effort, and fund-raising had been in vain. I had failed.

But I have found that when you decide to walk on water you will face moments of total despair. They are quitting points in your life that you must crash through in order to get to the other side of the miracle. That particular day was my quitting point. At times, it seems that when you take a leap of faith you fall into the abyss, and you think there's no way out. However, I have learned that an abyss is necessary. We think rock bottom is where dreams go to die. I have found that God re-creates you in those times into something you need to become to continue the journey.

The day I threw in the towel God decided to do something amazing. When I was overwhelmed by the devastating word *quit*, I just needed to trust Him.

I'm reminded how the prophet Elijah challenged the prophets of Baal in 1 Kings 18. Two altars were built and sacrifices prepared. Elijah gave the instructions: "Call on the name of your god, and I will call on the name of the LORD. The god who answers by setting fire to the wood is the true God!" (verse 24). The people who believed in and served the pagan gods prayed, danced, and even cut themselves for almost an entire day. Nothing happened. The silence was deafening. Their gods didn't so much as budge.

When it was Elijah's turn, he called out to God, and immediately the Lord answered, sending fire from the heavens and consuming the sacrifice. But that wasn't the only miracle that day. The fire was followed by a torrential downpour, God's end to a three-year drought that had devastated Israel, a miracle He had told Elijah days earlier would happen.

Elijah had walked on water. The prophet obeyed God to the point of risking his reputation and his very life. And God was faithful.

You would think that after experiencing these incredible supernatural acts, Elijah would have been empowered. But when he got word that Queen Jezebel planned on killing him, he reached his breaking point. Exhausted and pushed beyond his limits, the prophet wanted to give up and die. "'I have had enough, LORD,' he said. 'Take my life, for I am no better than my ancestors who have already died'" (1 Kings 19:4).

Although Elijah was ready to quit, God wasn't about to let him go. He gave the prophet enough strength to finish his journey (1 Kings 19:5-8).

God did the same for Matthew. As dejected as my husband initially felt, he did what he does best. He sprang into action and explored more creative and less expensive avenues of housing the residents of the Dream Center.

Obstacles will inevitably show up on your journey of walking on water. But in the midst of hardships or discouraging seasons, remember the One who is on your side. When you're tired from serving, ask God to renew your strength. "God said this once and for all; how many times have I heard it repeated? 'Strength comes straight from God'" (Psalm 62:11, *The Message*). When you don't have the funds you need to continue your ministry, trust God to provide. When you don't feel appreciated and you want to walk out, remember who you are really serving. When others tell you it's impossible for you to make a difference, remember in whom your confidence lies. Remind yourself of what another prophet wrote: "If you are walking in darkness, without a ray of light, trust in the LORD and rely on your God" (Isaiah 50:10).

Walking and Trusting Brings Miracles

As Matthew brainstormed, a Christian builder named Mike Rovner showed up. Before he crunched the numbers for his estimate, Mike met with all of the vendors and contractors who had expressed interest in the project. He gave them a personal tour of the facility, visiting every floor of every building on the Dream Center campus. They heard moving testimonies of people who shared where they came from, how they ended up at the Dream Center, and what God was doing in their lives. I've listened to stories like these for the past sixteen years, and they still make me tear up.

Putting faces with the stories touched the vendors' and contractors' hearts. Mike's proposal was $23 million less than our original estimate. That news gave Matthew the inspiration and strength he needed to hit the ground running and tackle the fund-raising.

When you have a God-sized dream or vision to help others, it will take more than your efforts, your talents, your time, your brain, your brawn, or your charm. It will take faith. It will take God. It will take you believing with confidence that you can walk on water.

I appreciate how God has purposely and beautifully designed the Dream Center in stages. If it was easy for us to pay the bills each month, we'd feel confident that we could get the job done on our own. We wouldn't have to rely on God with every ounce of strength and faith as we've had to do. If we didn't need generous donors who shared our vision, Matthew wouldn't have had the opportunity to travel all over the country telling others about God's faithfulness and inspiring them to change the world.

Provision Comes after We Start Walking

I believe financial burdens are a huge hindrance to people who are willing to step out in faith. How can I start a recreation center for the youth in my community or offer free meals at schools to children of low-income families or serve the needs of the elderly if I don't have a dime to my name?

These are legitimate questions. However, I've learned from my father-in-law that money follows ministry. In other words, answer the call and God will provide. This is not just a cliché. It's a formula we've used to create and build every ministry at the Dream Center. I've seen its truth in action every step of the way. If we had the money before we actualized our vision for meeting the different needs in the community, we never would have learned to trust God.

You don't get the money first and then become willing to do what God has called you to do. That wouldn't require faith or trust. That wouldn't require anything outside of human effort. You start the ministry and then God provides the money. Remember, the bills you accumulate by following His will are His to pay. He just needs a point person to be willing, take charge, and not give up.

As I've been working on this book, the Dream Center secured an incredible tax credit of $10.3 million. This means we will be able to finalize the renovations of the entire campus debt free. Not only that, we will also be able to expand the number of residents by 40 percent. This is a huge miracle and blessing not only to those who work at the Dream Center but also to the people we serve. It shows God's faithfulness when we are obedient to what He calls us to do.

Confidence Comes from Obedience

There is no better confidence booster than knowing you are living aligned with God's Word. When you are obedient to Scripture, God will bless what He has called you to do.

I think we can take a lesson from Joshua. After Moses' death, Joshua obediently stepped up to lead the nation of Israel into the Promised Land. This was a critical time in Israel's history. The promise God had made to Abraham centuries before was about to be fulfilled. Although God was involved in every detail of the conquest and had guaranteed victory for His chosen people, it wasn't going to be easy. Joshua had some huge obstacles ahead of him, most immediately the fact that the Canaanites had no plans to leave the land they had occupied for thousands of years.

As Joshua prepared for his new role, I imagine he had mixed emotions—feelings of excitement and anxiety. Then God spoke to him in a powerful way, encouraging the Israelite leader by offering certain promises if Joshua would fulfill God's spiritual expectations.

> Be strong and courageous, for you are the one who will lead these people to possess all the land I swore to their ancestors I would give them. . . . Be careful to obey all the instructions Moses gave you. Do not deviate from them, turning either to the right or to the left. Then you will be successful in everything you do. Study this Book of Instruction continually. Meditate on it day and night

so you will be sure to obey everything written in it. Only
then will you prosper and succeed in all you do.
JOSHUA 1:6-8

The next few chapters of the book of Joshua detail seemingly impossible obstacles that Joshua would overcome only
if he obeyed God's specific instructions. Joshua's first and only
job was to obey. God would do the rest and be faithful to His
promise.

When we live for God, we can trust that He has our best
interests in mind even as we contend with variables like trials,
uncertainty, and struggles. He knows what lies ahead on our
journey. When we face mountains that tower over us and seem
unsurpassable, if God tells us to start scaling them, we need to
obey. We can climb with confidence, knowing He will get us
over the top.

God's Fools

When my husband courageously stepped out in faith and
bought the hospital to expand the Dream Center, he didn't
have as much support as he'd hoped. Several pastors said he
was being irresponsible, and they refused to offer their resources
for something they were sure wouldn't last. The truth is, faith
looks risky and even foolish sometimes. But if you know you
are following God's plans, you have all the assurance you need
that things will ultimately work out one way or another. We've
seen that happen at the LA Dream Center and also at the New
York Dream Center started four years ago.

One volunteer at New York's Dream Center decided to be
obedient to God even though others thought she was out of
her mind. Coming from a horrible upbringing, she ultimately

trusted God to use her, and today she is on a journey to "help change the world."

Abuse and addiction—that's what I was born into. My parents went to church, but the things of this world looked so much better to them. Both were alcoholics and drug addicts. When my father was charged with rape and was sent to prison for fifteen years, my mom was left all alone with five children. My siblings and I went from shelter to shelter with a mother who was addicted to crack. Because of her addiction, we had no money. Because of her loneliness, she sought love in men. We were all forced to grow up fast. We moved into a hotel in downtown Los Angeles and that's when everything changed for me. I started doing drugs and living life my own way. I found myself ditching classes and falling behind in my first years of middle school.

Then I found the Dream Center—or maybe I should say the Dream Center found me. When I was twelve, I went to a youth winter retreat and God changed my life. I was able to finish high school at the age of sixteen. I was the first girl in my family to go to college. I worked as a teacher's assistant and then began teaching my own preschool class. When I was eighteen, I was asked to be the kindergarten teacher. I remember thinking that this was it, this was my dream. That's when God spoke to me about serving at the Dream Center in New York City.

As much as I fought against it, God began to open every door for me to go there. I wasn't the only one who questioned this move. Everyone was against me, even my own family. They thought I was crazy, but God had called me. Two years ago I moved to New York City. I run the Dream Center's children's ministry and help run the internship program. Though my journey hasn't been the easiest, God has never failed me. I'm not who I was; by the grace of God, I've been changed. Because I've been changed, it's my turn to help change this world, one day at a time.

Keep Your Motives in Check

You may know people who have said God told them to do something that ultimately didn't pan out. That might make you doubt what you think you hear from Him. I encourage you to keep your motives in check. If you feel God leading you to do something, ask yourself who it will help, who will receive glory, and why you feel you should do it. Then spend time studying Scripture and see if your desires line up with the Word of God. If you feel at peace after this self-evaluation, then march boldly into your commission.

I cannot judge people based on what they feel God has put in their hearts. I admit that I have struggled with and sometimes questioned other people's motives at times. While we cannot know for certain the root of ambition in the lives of others, we are responsible to gauge our own. When I signed up to be a volunteer, I jumped in 100 percent, wanting to do as much as I could to serve others. Six months later, I made the mistake of looking around and assessing how hard the other volunteers were working. Some of them were doing the bare minimum and still complaining about it!

I was confused. *Didn't we all sign up for the same thing—to change and save the world? Don't we all feel the same sense of urgency? Why am I working so hard if others aren't going to do the same?* In other words, I was being self-righteous and judgmental.

I quickly felt God tell me, *Keep your eyes on your own path and make sure you are obedient to what I am asking you to do. I am the One who has brought everyone here, and they are here for different reasons. If I have revealed a level of truth to you that they can't see yet, be thankful for it. I am working in their lives and I know their backgrounds and how far they have come. You are accountable to me for the truth I have allowed you to see.* Since that day, I've never judged anyone's level of commitment or compared how I serve to the way others do.

Don't scrutinize how willing, able, or committed someone else is. Assess your own motives for serving.

What's Shaking Your Confidence?

Any number of fears, worries, or obstacles can shake our confidence and stop us from believing that we can walk on water. Some people think they are too emotionally broken to be healed, let alone used by God. Others believe their life has been permanently damaged by evil, abuse, addiction, and other soul-scarring wounds. They feel they are not in a position, and never will be, to help others. Whatever the issue, it makes them doubt their usefulness.

For the last sixteen years, I have heard countless gut-wrenching testimonies from the people in our programs. Sons and daughters raped by their own fathers. Children finding their parents dead from a drug overdose. Children abandoned by their parents on a busy city street and left to survive alone. Lost children abducted and imprisoned, then sold as modern-day slaves.

It is almost impossible to believe that in the darkness of their adversity they found healing, wholeness, joy, and a future of hope and promise. But that's the good and merciful God we serve. He isn't satisfied with healing people's wounds just so they can merely survive life. He wants to transform people and give them a new identity so their suffering no longer marks them. He wants people to bring healing to others through the very story that bound them to shame.

You may feel God could never use you. Maybe your insecurities have overpowered your ability to believe. Maybe your story seems too far away from redemption. Maybe you think you've made too many mistakes. Maybe you just don't think you're capable of pulling off what you feel God is leading you to do. I want to encourage you to yield to God. Don't be afraid to say yes. Submit to Him and be His hands to hug the unloved, His mouth to speak His Word, His heart to love the hurting. Be His feet and walk on water.

Your Past Is Past

Matthew D., one of the leaders at the Dream Center, has faced a mountain of obstacles in his life, never imagining that God could use him as a leader. I hope his testimony inspires you as it has me. He shares:

I was born in Las Vegas into an extraordinary family of believers from all walks of life: professors, teachers, doctors, lawyers, actors, and evangelists. To put it mildly, the expectations were high. I was raised in Sin City, yet I was homeschooled, sheltered, and brought up to be a good Christian boy. I never really felt that I had a personal relationship with Christ. I was passionate about what others were passionate for, and ultimately this betrayed me. At thirteen, I rebelled, and by eighteen,

I was a drug addict. At twenty-four, I failed as a father with my precious children, Adryana, now thirteen, and Jiah, now eight.

The fighting between my wife and me was unbearable. She was a violent alcoholic and I was a lying and manipulative husband. The two of us created a toxic, abusive home environment. After seven years I left, leaving my kids behind. I was homeless at the age of twenty-seven and imprisoned for drugs at twenty-eight. Before my release, I asked the judge to let me stay in jail for another twelve months. I knew I needed that time to continue sobering up.

I had fallen quite far from my upbringing. Seemingly at the end of things, and while still in jail, I received an application in the mail to participate in the Dream Center discipleship program. There, I relished reading and memorizing Scripture daily and going to church.

Early on, I was placed in leadership and realized I had been called to serve all along. Even in my darkest days of heroin addiction, the Lord was still calling me. I was just too stubborn to listen.

One day I got up to speak to my group and it struck me: I had a passion to teach. Soon after, I was asked to take over the Education Department for Discipleship and serve on staff. Then I was asked to oversee the GED department, teaching and tutoring students who had never considered an education as something that they were entitled to.

I had found my great cause, my way to see justice served, my passion, my vision, my heartbeat, my fight, my outlet, and my calling. It was to teach and share a spiritual and moral recovery to many who were struggling in the same ways I had. I have never looked back.

Do I still struggle with the consequences of my past? Yes. But they do not define me. My future is bright and my legacy is building. My children and my family have been restored to me. My Creator and Savior is a friend who is real to me.

I know taking the first step to walk on water by serving others can be daunting, but I believe that in God's perfect timing you'll encounter a miracle. You'll find open doors of opportunity. You'll meet people to help you on your way. You'll find yourself face-to-face with the undeserved faithfulness of God. And before you know it, your doubts will begin to dissipate. Your insecurities will begin to vanish. Your fears will begin to crumble. And the water you will walk on will feel as secure as solid ground.

PART II

CONQUERING

How wonderful it is that nobody need wait a single

moment before starting to improve the world.

ANNE FRANK

CHAPTER 6

THE FEAR OF BEING UNWORTHY

He saved us, not because of righteous things we had done,
but because of his mercy. He saved us through the washing
of rebirth and renewal by the Holy Spirit.

TITUS 3:5, NIV

A FEW YEARS AGO, Matthew told me that the number one reason people will not step out in faith is because they feel unworthy. That blew me away.

But the more I thought about his statement, the more it made sense. Every day as I walk around the Dream Center campus, I come face-to-face with people who feel unworthy. I don't have to hear them utter the sentiment out of their mouths. I can just tell. Many of the women who are in the first thirty days of their addiction recovery program walk around with their heads held down. You sense their shame just by looking at them.

Something happens a few months down the road, however. They lift their heads higher. They start to smile. Even their posture improves. And many of them have a confidence they've never felt before.

The first question we ask a woman who enters our program at the Dream Center is, "What is your dream?" To most of them, it's a startling question. *Dream? What is that? You mean to actually do something positive?* They wonder how we can ask them to dream, to trust God, when they're simply struggling to make it day to day. They don't see dreaming as an option.

It's important that we challenge them to think outside of themselves and, most important, outside of their feelings of unworthiness. The Bible tells us that without a vision, people perish (Proverbs 29:18, KJV). If people don't have a dream, no plan to walk on water, their purpose or meaning is limited. They don't have a higher cause for which to live. When we challenge them to dream in spite of their feelings, suddenly things become possible. The cycle of shame starts to disappear and a new cycle begins, one that circles around confidence, dreams, and walking on water.

The Marks of Sin

Sin is Satan's greatest tool to make us feel unworthy. He likes to use the times we miss the mark to trap us, to make us stop trying to do the right things, or to shower us with shame so we merely survive, not thrive, in life. As a pastor's wife, I have the incredible opportunity to talk to many people. Often, they share their struggles with me. When I hear about their failures or mistakes, I don't judge them. I don't label them. I don't give up on them. I don't count them out or disqualify them from the race of faith.

I do, however, feel frustrated and think, *Shoot, they just tripped themselves again.* I know their lives could be so much better. They could experience more freedom, more healing, and more restoration if they didn't fall into the arms of temptation. I know this isn't the plan God has for them.

It's more than just sin that can cripple us. It's the mental and emotional gymnastics that go on as a result—like the over-powering feelings of guilt, shame, and brokenness. When we allow ourselves to drown in this cycle, we cannot do what God has called us to do. It's like God sending us out on a rescue operation to save people on a sinking boat. Our job is to pull people out of the water to safety, but instead we jump out of the boat and need to be rescued ourselves because we don't feel we are qualified to be rescue workers. So now God's boat has a smaller crew and even more people to rescue.

Not Feeling Good Enough

If it's not sin that makes us feel unworthy, it's the measuring stick we use to size up ourselves. Most of the time we allow other people to decide what the important benchmark for us is. But only God's opinion should really matter.

I love reading Max Lucado's book *You Are Special* to my kids. It has a powerful message. Punchinello is a Wemmick, a person carved out of wood. In the Wemmicks' world, what others think matters. Based on how they view their peers, they hand out gray dot stickers (bad) or gold stars (good) to each other. Sadly, Punchinello only gets gray dots. Then one day he meets Lucia, who doesn't have any stickers and couldn't care less. She tells Punchinello she spends time with Eli, the woodcarver who has created them all, and cares more about what he thinks.

Nobody other than God should decide your value. Sometimes we feel unworthy because of things that have happened to us. Many victims of sexual abuse, for example, struggle with shame. Many of the women at the Dream Center have shared with me that they even felt they deserved the abuse or asked for it. They carry the shame over the years and see themselves as permanently damaged or good for nothing. Oftentimes, their brokenness makes them shy away from serving others and making a difference.

Joyce never thought God would be able to use her because of abuse and addiction in her life. She shares,

> I was sexually abused by my grandfather throughout childhood. When I was twelve, I started smoking weed and drinking. By the time I was sixteen, I was shooting up heroin and cocaine. My addiction got worse as years went by. I did anything I could to get money for my dope. I robbed people, lied, and hurt and cheated everyone. I've been in and out of rehabs and jail and have lived on the streets. Before coming to the Dream Center, I was living on skid row.
>
> I have since completed the discipleship program and am working with the food truck. It amazes me that God is now using me to minister to hundreds of people every week. I pray for them and witness to them. I have been delivered from everything I used to be and everything that had held me back. I now have a purpose to live.

Don't let your insecurities and fear of not being good enough dictate if or how you allow God to use you. Maybe you don't think you read your Bible as often as your neighbor. Maybe you think you don't have enough faith. Maybe you think you've done some bad things in your life and God can't look past them and forgive you. Maybe your insecurities stem from not having a college degree.

Whatever the reason for your hesitance to take the first step, I challenge you to do it. I want you to believe with all your heart, not just in your head, that you are worthy to walk on water.

Even the Saints Felt Unworthy

Being worthy has nothing to do with being able to walk on water. Take Peter, for instance. As one of Jesus' inner circle, Peter was the first disciple who recognized that Jesus was the Messiah. He had walked with Him and had witnessed many miracles. Peter personally experienced the power of God through the authority Jesus gave him and the other disciples to cast out evil spirits and heal people afflicted with disease and illness.

In spite of the power Peter had, the miracles he saw, and the amazing opportunity to serve alongside Jesus, he disappointed the Lord. The disciple swore that he would never betray Jesus, but he denied Him three times just before Jesus' crucifixion. I believe Peter was sincere in his professed loyalty to Jesus, yet at the most critical moment he let Him down.

Just imagine. At the beginning of every day for the rest of his life, Peter would be reminded of his failures whenever a rooster crowed. Do you think for a minute that the disciple felt worthy of the call on his life? I don't think so.

If Peter hadn't repented and accepted Jesus' forgiveness, he would never have stepped back into ministry. He probably would have wasted away and lived a miserable life. But because Peter received the gift of grace that we have through the death of Jesus Christ, he was there to help build the early church. His sermon preached on the day of Pentecost resulted in three thousand new converts. Peter was spreading the gospel to Jews and Gentiles alike.

When you see what God accomplished through Peter despite his flaws and failures, you can see how important it is not to hide behind feelings of shame, regret, condemnation, disqualification, or unworthiness.

Peter wasn't the only powerful and influential person who

felt unworthy. Do you know what John the Baptist said? In referring to Jesus, John said, "I'm not even worthy to stoop down like a slave and untie the straps of his sandals" (Mark 1:7).

That's a pretty humble self-assessment. This is the same person of whom Jesus says later, "I tell you the truth, of all who have ever lived, none is greater than John the Baptist. Yet even the least person in the Kingdom of Heaven is greater than he is!" (Matthew 11:11). The same man honored by Jesus, the same man given the remarkable and unprecedented role of announcing the Messiah's arrival, is the same man who said he wasn't even worthy to untie the Lord's shoes. Did John think he was worthy to walk on water? Doubtful.

How about the apostle Paul? The man whose writings comprise almost half of the New Testament, one of the most well-known missionaries and accomplished church planters, also questioned his worth. He wrote to the church in Corinth, "I am the least of all the apostles. In fact, I'm not even worthy to be called an apostle after the way I persecuted God's church" (1 Corinthians 15:9). And yet Paul not only walked on water in his lifetime, he also gave his very life for the cause of faith.

Ready to Be Used?

If you are questioning your worth, you're not alone. But don't let it stop you from serving. God will work through you. Knowing that, you can boldly step out in faith and achieve the impossible.

If you've made mistakes and have repented, God can use you. If you didn't have the best education, God can use you. If you've been abused, mistreated, or neglected, God can use you. If you're a busy mom with three kids, God can still use whatever time you have available. If you're a high school student, you are not too young for God to use you. It doesn't matter who you are, where you're from, or what you've done—if you're willing to make a difference through a life of service, God can use you.

My friend Kenny had a tough life. He wrestled with the shame and guilt of his past and struggled with accepting that God could use him, even as he served in ministry. Here's how he ultimately found healing:

I am living the Scripture that says that those who are forgiven much love much.

For many years, I was so addicted to drugs and alcohol that I didn't care about anything or anyone. I lost everything, including my family and many friends. I'll never forget the night I got a call from a friend, begging me to pick her and her baby up because her boyfriend was high on drugs and going crazy. I arrived too late. The boyfriend had shot and killed my friend, her baby, and then himself.

After that, my life got worse. I didn't care about myself anymore; all I wanted was to die. I had been arrested so many times, the courts labeled me hopeless and crazy.

Yet my mother and sister never stopped praying for me. One day, my brother-in-law visited me in jail and asked me if I wanted to make a change. He told me about Jesus and how He wanted to love and forgive me. I was unsure about Jesus, but I did want a better life. Once I got out of jail, I went straight into Teen Challenge where I met and gave my life to Jesus. I completed the discipleship program, went on to Bible school, and became a children's pastor.

After living such a crazy life, it wasn't easy for me to think that God could ever really use me. I knew He loved me but I felt so underqualified and wanted to quit.

Eventually, I found healing in 1 Corinthians 1:27: "God chose things the world considers foolish in order to shame those who think they are wise. And he chose things that are powerless to shame those who are powerful." Yes, I was imperfect but God uses imperfect people to change the world. I started to experience God's unconditional love, forgiveness, and healing, which helped me move from the past to the present where I walk in God's confidence.

It's Not about Us

Walking on water isn't dependent on our abilities or know-how. We are able to do it through God alone. I don't know about you, but for me, this truth takes a lot of the pressure off. I don't have the power to heal. All I can do is pray and leave it to God to heal. I don't have the power to save souls. While I can tell someone about God, He must unveil the person's eyes.

I know I'm not called to do things outside of my spiritual giftings and that I don't need to force myself into an area of need in order to do God's job. I just have to make myself available and God will do the rest. He will perform the impossible miracle. As I've learned over and over again, half of a miracle is simply being where you are needed.

We are the channels God uses to show how great He is. That's why we can't take credit for the miracles that happen in people's lives that result from our service. We can't pat ourselves on the back and marvel at how amazing we are. We don't walk on water to add impressive accolades to our résumés. God gets the glory and is worthy of praise, honor, and worship; we are not. "Everything comes from him and exists by his power and is intended for his glory. All glory to him forever!" (Romans 11:36).

Though our faith should prompt us to do good things, God has to give us the power to get them done. The apostle Paul wrote, "We keep on praying for you, asking our God to enable you to live a life worthy of his call. May he give you the power to accomplish all the good things your faith prompts you to do. Then the name of our Lord Jesus will be honored because of the way you live, and you will be honored along with him. This is all made possible because of the grace of our God and Lord, Jesus Christ" (2 Thessalonians 1:11-12).

God has never asked us to be anything or do anything that He didn't fully intend to empower us to be or accomplish. So what's the point in shirking your responsibility? Why refuse to be His hands and feet?

More Evidence God Can Use You

If you're still hung up on wondering whether God can use you, here are three scriptural truths to help reshape your thinking.

- ‣ Everything is possible with God.
- ‣ He created you with care, with precision, with perfection, and with love.
- ‣ God desires everyone to be saved.

In Matthew 19:26 Jesus says, "Humanly speaking, it is impossible. But with God everything is possible." I like to think of this verse as the remedy to rid us of excuses and hang-ups. Jesus was talking to a rich man when he made this statement, telling him that though it is nearly impossible for one who has considerable wealth to enter heaven, it is possible with God. That's not the only thing that's possible when God enters the equation.

It is possible for you to accomplish that great challenge He is putting before you because you are a person of value and worth to God. Psalm 139 reminds us of that truth:

> You made all the delicate, inner parts of my body
> and knit me together in my mother's womb.
> Thank you for making me so wonderfully complex!
> Your workmanship is marvelous—how well I know it.
> You watched me as I was being formed in utter seclusion,
> as I was woven together in the dark of the womb.
> You saw me before I was born.
> Every day of my life was recorded in your book.
> Every moment was laid out
> before a single day had passed.
>
> How precious are your thoughts about me, O God.
> They cannot be numbered!
> I can't even count them;
> they outnumber the grains of sand!
> And when I wake up,
> you are still with me!
>
> PSALM 139:13-18

This passage of Scripture may be hard for you to swallow. You may find it difficult to believe that you are a marvelous creation of God's workmanship, wonderfully complex, and that God has precious thoughts about you. Isn't it great that God doesn't see us the same way we view ourselves? Did you know that He specifically designed you with certain abilities that would help serve others? Not only that, but He also instilled in you a unique passion so that you would enjoy doing those things!

It's obvious to me from studying the Bible that God doesn't handpick only certain people to use. He doesn't choose the most qualified, smartest, well-spoken, educated, or perfect people. Look at Peter. He was an uneducated fisherman with no formal religious training. He was brash and impulsive, often speaking before thinking. And he was used in remarkable ways to expand the Kingdom. God calls every one of us to serve others. He's got a job for each of us to do.

Finally, God is in the business of saving souls. John 3:17 tells us, "God sent his Son into the world not to judge the world, but to save the world through him." Above all else, He is concerned with the state of our souls. "What do you benefit if you gain the whole world but lose your own soul? Is anything worth more than your soul?" (Matthew 16:26).

Every ministry at the Dream Center is created for the ultimate purpose of saving souls. When we feed the hungry, we're not just satisfying a physical need—we are offering these people a reason to live, hope for tomorrow, the power to change, healing, and best of all, eternal salvation. Our food trucks are simply tools to meet people in their places of need. We hope that through our actions of love and representing Jesus through service, those in need will come to accept Him and live an abundant life for Him.

You Have What It Takes

I like to think of walking on water not in terms of worth, but in terms of qualifications. What qualifies us to accomplish God's will?

When I was brand new at the Dream Center, I remember venting to God during one particular prayer time. I complained that I wasn't gifted or talented enough, that I lacked the abilities I thought I needed to be used of Him.

I was scared to death of public speaking, often shaking and stumbling on my words. I disqualified myself from teaching Bible studies because I didn't think I had the knowledge or skills. I couldn't sing solos and had terrible stage fright. When I was growing up, these visible gifts seemed like the most important roles of ministry in the church. Without any of them, I couldn't see how I could be useful at all.

God reminded me of 1 Corinthians 13. There, Paul reminds believers that love is the greatest gift in ministering to others. In that moment, God spoke to my heart saying, *Caroline, the greatest ability you can possibly have is the gift of love.*

His words lifted my spirit. I immediately felt empowered, not in my own abilities, but because of the love He has given me for people. I thank God that He taught me this truth early on. I finally believed that I could be used powerfully.

This doesn't mean that I don't work on developing other areas in my life. I applied the Word of God to help me overcome my fear of speaking in front of people; I didn't want to waste the platform and gifting God has given me to rally people around a cause. I studied the Bible so I could better communicate His Word.

Love Is the Key

I love the way *The Message* paraphrases 1 John 3:18-22:

> My dear children, let's not just talk about love; let's practice real love. This is the only way we'll know we're

living truly, living in God's reality. It's also the way to shut down debilitating self-criticism, even when there is something to it. For God is greater than our worried hearts and knows more about us than we do ourselves.

And friends, once that's taken care of and we're no longer accusing or condemning ourselves, we're bold and free before God! We're able to stretch our hands out and receive what we asked for because we're doing what he said, doing what pleases him.

It's true! When I love on someone—whether serving in an outreach or working on a project to build the community—my negative thoughts about myself or anyone else disappear. I don't focus on my insecurities. I don't think about what I don't have to offer. I don't compare myself with others.

In those moments, life seems bigger than my feelings. My insecurities seem small and irrelevant. The presence of God fills up the moment. I see Him at work through the faces of those I serve. I feel complete and whole, knowing that I am doing what I am called to do. God doesn't command us to serve others to burden us, but to help us enjoy the life we have. It brings me personal peace, joy, and a deep love I would otherwise have never known.

Can you love people?

Do you have a heart for others?

If the answer to these questions is yes, guess what? You are qualified to serve.

From Being Broken to Being Used

Michael Conner, our discipleship director at the Dream Center, went through a season of feeling unworthy. Despite his situation he decided to take God at His Word and seek Him for an opportunity to serve. When God opened the door, Michael didn't let his own feelings of inadequacies stop him:

> I came from a very strict Pentecostal upbringing, went to Bible college, and became a preacher just like my father and my grandfather. Life was good. I held revivals and made a difference wherever I spoke. I met and married who I thought was the girl of my dreams.
>
> In order to live the American Dream, I got a "real" job in retail, but continued doing ministry on the side. My dream turned into a nightmare. My wife, who had been only a recent convert to Christ when we were married, became frustrated with being a preacher's wife. After nine years, she decided to call it quits. I was devastated and thought my ministry was over.
>
> I switched churches and started attending one that followed the model of Phoenix First Assembly. The leaders there nurtured me back to spiritual health and I resumed ministry, not in the pulpit but with real people who had real hurts and real needs.
>
> I loved serving others. My pastor liked to say that I worked a full-time job to support my habit of ministry. Eventually I started working at a homeless shelter and found myself back in full-time ministry. I fell in love with a woman who was serving with me in ministry at our local church and we decided to marry.
>
> Life was good again! But a year later, we divorced. To say the least, it was another absolutely crushing blow. I thought I was somehow cursed by God to never be happy, to never do ministry, and to never make a

difference in other people's lives because I couldn't get my own life together.

I had signed up for pastor school and decided to still attend, hoping that somehow I could receive word from God about what to do with my life. To be honest, it wasn't a very happy time for me. I remember sitting up in the top balcony and looking down at the staff section, wondering and hoping that maybe someday, in spite of all my failures, I could be on staff at a church like this. I dismissed it as wishful thinking.

When I returned home, I finally began to realize I didn't have to be a perfect Christian. I humbled myself before God and told Him I was His to use anyway, anywhere He wanted me to go.

A year later, I was asked to take over the discipleship program at the Dream Center. Never in my wildest dreams did I see that coming. I didn't personally know the Barnetts and they didn't know me. It was a total God thing. After years of trying to do something great for God, it was the faithfulness in the small things that finally paid off. I stepped out of my comfortable boat and started walking on water, and my life has never been the same.

I asked God's forgiveness for all of my mistakes that contributed to the brokenness I had found myself in during those dark, lonely days. He has forgiven me and restored so much more than what I ever gave up or lost.

I believe Mike's own season of brokenness is what makes him so powerful in helping other people find their healing. He knows the pain of regret, and yet his life is a moving example that you can walk boldly into your future with God because He truly loves and forgives and forgets.

Positively Powerful

When I was a little girl, my mom was always quick to correct me if she overheard me making fun of someone. "Caroline," she'd say, "you should never criticize someone God made." Of course, she was right.

In the same vein, how dare we question how God made us? How dare we challenge His creation? We have no business calling what God calls righteous, unrighteous. Or loved, unlovable. Or capable, incapable. Or fearfully and wonderful made, ugly or worthless. So stop putting yourself down. Stop minimizing your talents. Stop focusing on your unworthiness.

When we redirect our energy into something positive, we become less self-absorbed. Instead of wallowing in self-pity or doubt, do something good for someone else. Reroute your negative feelings into acts of service, big or small. For instance, if you find yourself focusing on your weakness, buy lunch for someone in need. Instead of thinking about the sin you were forgiven for years ago, pray for a troubled youth in your church or community. Instead of complaining that you're unqualified, visit a nursing home and spend time with the elderly.

And remember: you are not worthy to walk on water because of what you have or have not done. You are worthy only because of what Christ has done for you.

CHAPTER 7

NOT WILLING TO SINK

Let's not get tired of doing what is good.
At just the right time we will reap a harvest
of blessing if we don't give up.

GALATIANS 6:9

WHEN YOU SAY YES to walking on water, you must immediately resolve that sinking is not an option. You won't quit. You won't give up. You won't miss your chance to show the world who God is through your acts of service. This isn't something you conclude as your foot is in midair, ready to get wet. Or when you're flying halfway across the world to serve on the mission field. Or when you submit your paperwork to be a foster parent. It must be a predetermined, nonnegotiable stipulation. You are not going to give yourself an out.

Peter had the great privilege of being the poster child for God's limitless abilities. His walk on water showed us that God can override the laws of physics and nature. But the minute the disciple took his eyes off of Jesus and looked around, Peter was struck with fear. He realized he was doing something that was impossible. He started focusing inward, at his own inabilities and insecurities, instead of continuing to trust in Jesus with the same faith he had to get out of the boat in the first place. Peter became overwhelmed and gave up.

People sink for many reasons. They may give up serving others because they're not sure they have enough faith to keep up the fight. They may think that what they set out to do is too hard. They may quit because they don't see immediate results. They may feel stretched too thin, juggling too many priorities with a life of service. Whatever the reason, the resulting frustration and stress can make anyone feel miserable and want to give up.

Rely on God

When we try to manage our lives and serve others in our own strength, we run a race that's impossible to win. The only way to achieve the goal is to start each day with God's hope and end each day with His peace. I'm not talking about setting aside time out of your day to have devotions and commune with God, though those things are obviously important to do and will benefit your faith walk. I'm talking about intentionally assessing and, if need be, shifting your perspective when you wake up and when you lay your head down at night.

Of course, we must focus on the right things not only at the beginning and end of each day. In the hours between, we must rely on God's strength and guidance. It's important to live each day in godly wisdom. When times get tough and we feel discouraged, confused, or afraid, we must press into God and remember that "when [we are] weak, then [we are] strong" (2 Corinthians 12:10, NIV).

As I've begun to intentionally start and end the day with God, I've seen tremendous changes in my attitude and my effectiveness. Let me share some of what I've learned.

A Day That Begins with Hope

Beep-beep-beep-beep. The alarm sounds and rouses you from a deep sleep. Maybe you groan and hit the snooze button. Maybe you turn it off and hit the ground running. The one thing I'm sure you do is start thinking of the list of things you have to do today. *Make a final review of the morning's presentation before the board. Take the baby to the doctor. Meet with the bank lender. Research senior living facilities for Mom.*

Sometimes we wake up with worry; concerns weigh heavily on our mind. We are anxiously wondering about the results of a lab report from the doctor. Or who our daughter was with last night. Or how we're going to pay our mortgage this month. I tend to wake up thinking about the various people I know and am praying for. Like the father who desperately needs a job so he and his family won't get evicted. Or the girl I met at church who is having second thoughts about staying in the discipleship program.

Our minds are inundated with a nonstop barrage of responsibilities, worries, expectations, concerns, and prayers that affect almost every aspect of our lives. That's exactly why it's crucial that we start each day with God's hope. We deliberately remind ourselves that God is in control of everything; that we must cast our cares on Him; that we must remember He has the power to change people and situations. Read this beautiful passage from Scripture:

> God proves to be good to the man who
>   passionately waits,
>   to the woman who diligently seeks.
> It's a good thing to quietly hope,
>   quietly hope for help from God.

It's a good thing when you're young
 to stick it out through the hard times.

When life is heavy and hard to take,
 go off by yourself. Enter the silence.
Bow in prayer. *Don't ask questions:*
 Wait for hope to appear.
Don't run from trouble. Take it full-face.
 The "worst" is never the worst.

Why? Because the Master won't ever
 walk out and fail to return.
If he works severely, he also works tenderly.
 His stockpiles of loyal love are immense.
He takes no pleasure in making life hard,
 in throwing roadblocks in the way.

LAMENTATIONS 3:25-33, *The Message* (EMPHASIS ADDED)

As soon as you get up in the morning, take a deep breath and start thanking God. Thank Him for His faithfulness, for His love, for His grace, for your family, for your health, for anything you can think of. Then think of an area where you need to be strengthened with His hope and find relevant Scriptures to meditate upon. For example, if you have been concerned and faithfully praying for a family member to know God, repeat Acts 16:31 out loud, thanking God in advance that he or she will be saved. If you are hoping for a promotion or a raise at work, stand on the promise of John 15:7. If you need provision in your ministry, speak the words of 1 Thessalonians 5:24. Purposefully digging into Scripture will bring hope where you need it the most.

Hoping for Change

Maintaining hope is especially important when you start working with and helping hurting people. When you try to help better people's lives, you'll typically find yourself desperately wishing they would change—and quickly.

You hope that certain obstacles in their lives—getting an education or a job, recovering from addiction, healing from hurt, creating a life of independence—would be overcome sooner rather than later. The problem is, change takes time. Not only that, but it is God who ultimately brings change.

It's easy to get discouraged when people don't recover as fast as we want them to. The temptation to sink becomes great. I discovered this working at the Dream Center. People who come to our organization for help enter an intense one-year live-in discipleship program. They are taught to confront and overcome their issues by learning to create positive coping techniques based on biblical principles. They must participate in a regimented work therapy program, group and individual Bible study, and outreaches. Sometimes you can tell who is going to make it and who is not.

I remember one young man with a history of addiction who entered our program. He was polite and respectful and didn't look as physically spent as most drug addicts who come to us. Judging from the outside, I thought he had a pretty good chance of graduating the program and making it in life. Yet much to my surprise, several months later he quit.

A few months after that he returned, but this time he looked beaten down and ragged. Whatever he had been through on the streets had taken a huge toll on his physical appearance and his demeanor. Once again, after a few months in the program, he split.

A couple of weeks later, I was in the car waiting for the light to change at a major intersection near the campus when I saw this young man panhandling on the side of the road. I almost didn't recognize him. He had lost a significant amount of weight and looked like he had aged twenty years. His face was bruised and swollen, as if he had just gotten into a fight.

I was devastated and heartbroken, and my hope for him dropped. *Why had he given up? What convinced him that whatever he was doing on the streets was better than a life of wholeness and health? Could we have done more for him? Had we failed him somehow?*

I saw him several more times at that same intersection. One time, I rolled down my window and called out his name. He walked over to my car. "We'd really like to see you again at the Dream Center. Would you consider coming back?" I asked.

"Not to discipleship," he replied, informing me that he didn't have an addiction. "I'm doing fine. I only have to panhandle two hours a day to get enough money for a room and food for the day. I don't need any help."

I realized drugs weren't his problem. He had a root issue—pride. That's what was keeping him from pursuing a better life.

It can be discouraging when you spend weeks, months, even years serving, helping, and loving on someone without seeing any fruit. It's downright disappointing. I have seen so many volunteers quit because they get disillusioned when they've spent so much time helping people who then don't make it. The volunteers question whether the commitment is worth it.

You may not see immediate changes. When you get discouraged, here is something important to remember: one day, when you give an account before God, He will focus on how you made yourself available to be used by Him, not the results of answering the call. It's not your job to produce the fruits of your labor. That's God's job. Your job is to be willing to walk on water.

Our first discipleship director was once asked, "What is the success rate of the program?" He responded, "One hundred percent." The person who asked the question laughed. "That's impossible." To which the director replied, "No, it's true. Because God's Word never returns void." What a brilliant answer. Don't worry if you don't see immediate fruits of every seed you plant or every effort you make. Just trust God to bring about change according to His timing.

Heidi started working with a ministry that had its share of challenges. She almost gave up because the fruits of her efforts were not immediately seen. She learned the end result is in God's hands. She testified,

I work with ladies who have been so used and abused that they have learned the pattern of using and abusing to survive. I've watched them give in to the lie over and over again, and have occasionally been trapped in the middle of it.

When that happens, it leaves me feeling like I have poured everything I have into helping them overcome the lie, and then got burned in the process. I feel like I have nothing else to offer, and I want to give up. In those moments, I have spent some sweet, intimate prayer times with Jesus. Each time, He reminds me of the privilege I have to work for Him, and that instills hope in me, knowing that He wins at the end.

I know that the Lord cares so much more about the people in my world than I ever can, and He is so much more concerned with what happens to them than I can even imagine. It is His love for us and His belief in His beloved children, not my love for people, that gives me the grace to keep going.

Miraculous Outcomes

For every person who leaves the Dream Center without reaching recovery, there are many others who do. Their stories inspire me to keep up the good fight of faith. Sarai's journey is one example:

When I was about nine years old, my mom married a man that my brother and I didn't know anything about. My brother didn't approve of the relationship and started acting out and rebelling. He ended up getting kicked out of the house. At that time, my stepdad started sexually abusing me. I was thirteen when I finally got the courage to tell my mom what my stepdad was doing to me. She called me a liar and every other name in the book. After that, I don't remember ever feeling safe in my own home again.

In the summer of 2007 we went on vacation to California. The night we were heading home, my stepdad beat me so bad I ended up in the hospital. I woke up surrounded by police officers and a social worker. My mom and stepdad had left me behind in California. I ended up in the foster-care system.

My first foster home was in Watts, California, where I would cry myself to sleep every night. One of the girls in the home introduced me to crystal meth. The drug took over my life. I felt nothing and I cared about no one. But I no longer cried. I started selling drugs and partying all the time. I ran away from group homes and foster homes and dropped out of high school.

One day I met a guy who was a Christian. We started dating. When he found out about my drug addiction, he started to talk to me about God and the Bible. I got really upset and ended up breaking up with him. For some reason, he didn't give up on me. He called me every day and gave his pastor my number too. He invited me to his church. I went, but I was high.

One evening, I went to a "testimony night" at the church. I couldn't stop listening to the people talk about God and how He had changed their life. They were so happy. I knew that I wanted what they had. That night I told the pastor what was going on in my life and that I was ready to give it all up.

I entered the discipleship program at the Dream Center soon after. God has brought restoration to my family and me. I got my GED, and God has placed a dream in my heart to work with the children in the foster-care system. My life has changed drastically, and I will never turn back.

If you don't start your day with hope in God, you're closer to sinking than walking. Whatever troubles you or weighs you down, know that God is your hope in and for all things.

Recharge When You Need To

It's easy to get overwhelmed, but it's just as easy to rest in God. When you find yourself feeling discouraged in your service to others, tired from the hard work your ministry requires, or even stressed from trying to juggle a life of service with a personal life, take a break. Take five minutes out of your day and find a quiet place to get back into the presence of God. Decompress emotionally by recharging spiritually. Remind yourself of how big God is and how small the worry, problem, or task is in comparison.

Frankly, I think we all need about a five-minute break a few times throughout the day to gain God's strength and refocus our attention on the right things. It will be more beneficial than venting to a friend or colleague about how stressful your situation is.

If you decide not to cast your daily cares on God, you are saying that they are too big for Him. If you step back, however, and release your anxieties and allow Him to saturate you with hope, He will lighten your load and carry your burdens for you.

End Your Day with God's Peace

Forget about spending a weekend at a spa or going on a juice fast. I've discovered the best spiritual and mental detox is to end my day with God's peace. When I come home after a long day at work, I spend time with my family, feed and bathe the kids, clean up, answer some e-mails, and finally get ready for bed. I take a deep breath and start talking to God, telling Him about some things that may have hurt, disturbed, or frustrated me in my walking-on-water journey that day. Some days I'm so physically and emotionally worn out from the day's events, I can only manage to repeat, "Thank You for Your peace," ten or twenty times.

I'm not tied to a certain length of prayer time. I just pray for however long it takes to feel peace. Some days it takes longer than others because I've got more on my mind. If I spend enough time with God, I can feel the peace that passes under-standing even in the middle of a great storm.

I confess I haven't always put this into practice. For eight years, I couldn't sleep without popping a pill. I tried every sleep aid available, from over-the-counter drugs to prescriptions. Nothing did the trick. I could never get a full night's rest. Every night for two or three hours, I'd lie awake staring at the ceiling. I'd think. And worry. And fret. And wonder. And worry some more.

Oh, I knew about God's peace. I knew that Jesus left His followers this promise: "I am leaving you with a gift—peace of mind and heart. And the peace I give is a gift the world can-not give. So don't be troubled or afraid" (John 14:27). I knew I needed to trust God because He is bigger than my problems. However, I didn't make the connection in my heart.

Consequently, I wasn't releasing my life to God every day. Scripture says that each day has its own share of worries (Matthew 6:34). I was guilty of lugging around days' and even weeks' worth of accumulated worries. I was guilty of carry-ing yesterday's burdens into today, and today's burdens into tomorrow.

Turning head knowledge into heart knowledge is actually very practical. It's not about shifting your feelings. It's about taking control of your mind. This takes daily practice. I made the choice to believe, no matter how I felt, that God was in control and that He would take care of all things. I wasn't going to allow myself to get swept up in worry or fear.

I prayerfully lifted up every negative and faith-crippling thought or concern that came my way and gave them to God. Eventually, prayer by prayer, I experienced more peace, until I finally started believing His truth with all my heart.

WILLING TO WALK ON WATER

Once I began ending my day with God's peace, I slept like a baby. I didn't toss and turn. I didn't need any more sleep aids. I could even have a cup of regular coffee in the late afternoon without worrying about it keeping me awake all night.

When you start walking on water, it's not enough to just know the fundamental truth about God. You have to make up your mind and believe it with all your heart. You have to live it. You have to experience it. This is what will keep you from sinking.

How to Do It

End your day with peace the same way you start your day with hope. Thank God for how good, loving, kind, merciful, and wonderful He is. Spend time in the Word. Apply Scripture to the worries you have and allow the peace of God, which passes understanding, to wash over you. And remember the words of the apostle Paul: "Don't worry about anything; instead, pray about everything. Tell God what you need, and *thank him* for all he has done. Then you will experience God's peace, which exceeds anything we can understand. His peace will guard your hearts and minds as you live in Christ Jesus" (Philippians 4:6-7, emphasis added).

Do the Work

It takes work to maintain peace. Paul wrote, "The Scriptures say, 'If you want to enjoy life and see many happy days . . . turn away from evil and do good. Search for peace, and work to maintain it'" (1 Peter 3:10-11).

I recently uncluttered our home. After four years of letting stuff accumulate in our house without any rhyme or reason, my work was cut out for me. It took a few days, but I went through every drawer, cabinet, bin, and box in every room, including the garage. I tossed out junk, made piles of stuff to donate, and organized the rest. I threw myself into the project, but at times it seemed like a daunting task. When it was done, I was proud of how things looked. Every item had a place of its own, where it belonged. If I may say so myself, I did a pretty good job.

Today my house is very low maintenance. I can tidy up in less than three minutes at the end of each day. If I keep this up daily, hopefully I won't have to declutter the house for another few years. I'll be able to live in peaceful order, not organized chaos.

The same principle applies to our relationship with God. If it's been a long time since you've experienced His peace, I'm willing to bet that you've been carrying baggage from days, weeks, or months. Maybe even longer. You might find remnants of bitterness from that fight you had with your sister five years ago. You might discover residual anger from the raise you didn't get last month. You might even stumble over a garbage bag of disappointment from that unanswered prayer for something that you desperately thought you deserved. Over time, disappointments and stresses pile up in every corner of your life, taking up so much room, there is virtually no more space for peace to slip in.

Take those sins, burdens, and worries to God. Be honest with Him. Allow Him to remove them. Peace might not happen immediately, but I promise it will come. And don't stop doing this after just one night. Make it a habit. Make it a part of your evening routine, like brushing your teeth.

Make room for God to fill you with the peace only He can give. "In peace I will lie down and sleep, for you alone, O LORD, will keep me safe" (Psalm 4:8). If you don't start your day with God's hope and end your day with His peace, you are setting yourself up to sink.

Don't Take Your Eyes off Jesus

I appreciate what the apostle Paul wrote in Philippians 4:8-9, but sometimes I find it difficult to understand. "And now, dear brothers and sisters, one final thing. Fix your thoughts on what is true, and honorable, and right, and pure, and lovely, and admirable. Think about things that are excellent and worthy of praise. Keep putting into practice all you learned and received from me—everything you heard from me and saw me doing. Then the God of peace will be with you."

Most of what I see on a daily basis isn't pure, lovely, or admirable. In fact, it's unjust, unpleasant, and impure. I am passionate about eliminating social injustice because I am outraged at how many men, women, and children are homeless and living on the streets; the number of sexually explicit billboard signs; and the rundown and dangerous neighborhoods where children live and play.

In these verses, Paul wasn't telling us to ignore the harsh reality of evil in this world. He was reminding us to turn our attention off of those horrible things and toward the things that are true and honorable. Jesus is true and honorable. He is the great *I AM*. He will never lie to us, let us down, or disappoint us. If we fix our eyes on Jesus, we are guaranteed never to sink.

Paula has lived this truth through times of tragedy, torment, and uncertainty. Instead of focusing on her trials, she has learned to continually look to the One who has pulled her through. She shares,

> When I was seven years old, my mom left my dad, and
> in turn, my dad left the state and never had a hand in
> raising me. My mom married repeatedly and by the time
> I was fourteen, I had had four fathers, one of whom

sexually abused me for years. By eighteen, I had moved eighteen times. Despite living in such an environment, I learned to depend on the Lord.

After I graduated from college, I got married. When I became pregnant with our first child, everything was great until the fifth week. The hormonal changes I was undergoing altered my brain chemically, and I became depressed and suicidal. I spent most of my pregnancy in a psychiatric unit of a hospital.

By God's grace I was able to focus on God's promise to give me the desire of my heart, which was a baby. Each day the torment of depression grew, but my hope in Jesus grew as well. It was a supernatural and unexplainable hope. I gave birth to a healthy, full-term baby boy. I was completely healed of my depression and did not experience even a hint of postpartum depression. I was a miracle, and so was my baby.

After our son was a year old, we met with our doctors and decided to try for a second child. Unfortunately, during my second pregnancy, I became even more depressed than the first time. I tried to kill myself three times. Because I was a risk to myself and the baby, I was again admitted to the hospital. God had miraculously saved my first baby and me, so I focused on Him. Two years and three months after our first son was born, we welcomed another healthy boy. Both sons are living miracles, attesting to the faithfulness of God.

In the summer of 2008, I was diagnosed with breast cancer. A month later, my husband was diagnosed with stage-four colon cancer. Our sons were fourteen and twelve at the time. I vividly remember the horror of having to tell the boys that both their parents had cancer.

Over the next two years, my husband and I battled our cancers together. My communion with the Lord was unceasing. There wasn't a thought or situation that I didn't entrust to God. He was my focus, not the cancer. My husband lost his battle two years later. Once again I looked to the One who had proved to be exactly what He claimed to be—all sufficient; the one and only person I could count on always. On my knees, I continued to seek God to meet our needs. Little by little, the miracles continued and the answers came.

Life hasn't been easy, but in learning to shift my attention to Jesus, I have experienced and come to truly know His faithfulness, His sustaining grace, His miraculous provision, and His never-ending love and compassion. I am totally dependent on Him.

Guard your thoughts and keep them centered on the One who is capable of healing the maimed, defending the widows and orphans, restoring the lost, and redeeming the broken. Rejoice over the good that God has brought into your life and to those around you and allow it to sink in.

Think about how God is at work in the world. In the alcoholic who is now sober after twenty years. In the loving parents who have adopted a child from a third-world country. In the youth group that has raised enough money to provide clean water for a village in Africa.

When you start to think about the good things God is doing, your faith walk will get stronger.

CHAPTER 8

YOUR MOTIVATING FACTOR

Nothing can ever separate us from God's love. Neither death nor life, neither angels nor demons, neither our fears for today nor our worries about tomorrow—not even the powers of hell can separate us from God's love. No power in the sky above or in the earth below—indeed, nothing in all creation will ever be able to separate us from the love of God that is revealed in Christ Jesus our Lord.

— ROMANS 8:38-39 —

AFTER PETER HAD DENIED JESUS, he went back to his former job as a fisherman, probably assuming Jesus couldn't use him anymore. But Jesus had not given up on Peter.

When Mary arrived at the empty tomb, the angel of the Lord told her to go and tell the disciples "including Peter" (see Mark 16:7) that He had risen from the dead. What a gift to Peter! Jesus singled him out by name, showing Peter that he had never been disqualified from ministry. I imagine Peter must have been overjoyed, released from any guilt he still carried when he heard the good news. Later, Jesus sat with Peter and asked him a series of questions.

"Simon son of John, do you love me more than these?"

"Yes, Lord," Peter replied, "you know I love you."

"Then feed my lambs," Jesus told him.

Jesus repeated the question: "Simon son of John, do you love me?"

"Yes, Lord," Peter said, "you know I love you."

"Then take care of my sheep," Jesus said.

A third time he asked him, "Simon son of John, do you love me?"

Peter was hurt that Jesus asked the question a third time. He said, "Lord, you know everything. You know that I love you."

Jesus said, "Then feed my sheep."

JOHN 21:15-17

Why the repetition? I believe that Jesus wanted to clarify for Peter that his motivation for going out and reaching the lost and helping those in need had to be birthed out of his love for Jesus. His work to further the Kingdom of God was not a means to pay penance for his sin or to make up for denying the Messiah. Otherwise, I think Jesus would have asked Peter if he felt bad for messing up.

If we understood at a deep level the awe-inspiring and life-changing love God has for us, a lot of our decisions would be different. Our lives would be better. I believe there are people in hell who would say, "If I had known then how much God loved me, I would have lived a different life. I would have followed God." I look forward to understanding God's love for me in heaven. I'm sure I'll realize how silly my hang-ups were—like my insecurity and fear of rejection—and how I wasted time fretting over them. Possibly even the great heroes of the faith will realize they could have taken bigger risks or had fewer doubts.

As you live day to day and serve others, your number one motivator must be God's love for you. His love should compel you to get up in the morning. His love should inspire you to make a difference. His love should move you to forgive, show grace, and extend mercy. His love should compel you to be a better man, woman, leader, teacher, caregiver, friend.

Facets of God's Love

The best definition of God's love is found in 1 Corinthians 13:4-7:

> Love is patient and kind. Love is not jealous or boastful or proud or rude. It does not demand its own way. It is not irritable, and it keeps no record of being wronged. It does not rejoice about injustice but rejoices whenever the truth wins out. Love never gives up, never loses faith, is always hopeful, and endures through every circumstance.

I once conducted an exercise at one of our women's meetings. I read the 1 Corinthians 13 definition of love several times, then asked the women to think how they loved different individuals in their lives. First, I asked them to think about their children. "It's easy to think of your kids lovingly, isn't it?" I remarked. "Okay. How about your husband? Do you love him according to this definition?" Some of the women hesitated at the "keeps no record of being wronged" phrase, but overall they agreed.

"How about yourself?" A number of the women in the group started crying as their raw emotions surfaced. Many people have a hard time loving themselves, feeling they fall short of God's definition of love.

I read the verses one last time. "Now think about how God, your heavenly Father, loves you." It was impossible for some of the women to accept this truth. I prayed for God to work through these broken hearts so they could come to a true understanding of how He loved them so deeply and so personally.

Spend a few minutes doing this exercise on your own. Read this Scripture out loud and think of your kids, your spouse or loved one, yourself. Now focus on God's love for you. Do you believe He loves you that deeply? Do you accept this definition of His love for you? Do you live each day knowing His love for you is patient? Kind? Forgiving? Hopeful? Enduring, no matter the situation?

Take It Personally

My primary mission in life is to approach every endeavor, big and small, from the attitude and knowledge that God personally loves me. I know if I can accomplish this, I can accomplish every desire of my heart. It can be challenging at times. It's easy to fall back into a mind-set of fear and insecurity, feeling defeated, incapable, and quite simply, unworthy of God's love.

I find it's much easier to believe God loves people collectively than to apply His love to me personally. It took me a long time to believe in my heart and accept that God loves Caroline Barnett, even though I grew up in a loving, affectionate family and church. I knew God loved me. I even sang songs and read Bible verses about it. But as I got older, understanding and embracing God's love wasn't quite as simple. I tiptoed around that truth, unsure of what to expect. I was almost suspicious that I didn't have to earn or even deserve it.

When Human Love Fails

Unless we understand that God loves us personally, we'll never "get it" and we'll always question it.

There are many reasons people struggle with accepting God's love. I believe our perception of God often stems from how our earthly fathers treated us or exemplified love. If you had a dad who was abusive, mean, hurtful, or unloving, you may have a tough time accepting that God's love is good.

One Thursday night at the close of our church service, the guest speaker invited anyone who hated their father to come forward for prayer. Almost six hundred people made their way to the altar. I was shocked.

My friend Aaron is someone who had a skewed view of God because of his earthly father. Yet he ultimately learned about and came to accept the loving nature of God. He says,

When I was young, my father was my hero. I had no problem associating an eternal Father's love with a natural father's love. But as I grew older and became more aware of the way my father's absence affected our family, I had a hard time believing that his actions were loving.

I began to question how I could ever accept God's eternal love when God gave me an earthly father who was incapable of showing me love. Did God really love me if He allowed these things to happen?

I tried my best to prove that I deserved His love, and when I fell short of my expectations, I was convinced that He was on His way out the door. I believed that the God who created me had given up on me and that if He didn't love me, I had no chance in life.

It was in this rock-bottom moment of depression that God revealed Himself to me. When I finally put my trust in Him, He did not remind me of my previous mistakes or scold me for my bad behavior. He simply picked me up and told me that there was nothing I could do to make Him leave. He told me that I had a future and that I was no longer bound to the ideas left in my head by my father. In my time of weakness, God revealed the love of a true Father to me.

You Can't Earn God's Love

I'm thankful to have a great relationship with my dad. I love him and look up to him. He is a loving, kind, godly, and gentle man.

Though I never felt I had to earn my dad's love, I felt I had to earn God's love. Perhaps it's because God knows me inside and out. He knows what I'm thinking. He knows my desires, my intentions, my inner battles, and my judgments. I can't fake it with God. I can pretend I'm good enough or "together" for others, but they can't read my mind and see my true intentions and motivations. Only God can.

In February 2011 I was invited to speak at a women's conference, the day after my father-in-law's annual Pastors and Leaders School. My plan was to devote the week before the event to studying the Word and praying an hour a day. I wanted the power of God to flow through me and minister to those who attended the conference. I felt in order for God to show up in such a big and mighty way, I had to invest my time, energy, and effort into making that happen.

Unfortunately, things didn't go as planned. I was helping teach workshops in the pastors and leaders conference. It was exciting but also exhausting.

I had been pulled in so many different directions that I hardly studied or prayed at all for the women's conference. That morning, I holed myself up in my room and cried like a baby. I felt guilty, ashamed that I had not kept my commitment. I prayed in between sobs, begging God to forgive me. "I let you down," I cried. "I'm not worthy to be used to minister to these women."

I heard God speak to my heart. *Caroline, had you spent that time in the Word and in prayer, would that have qualified you to serve me? Would that have made you worthy? Daughter, even at your best, you are not worthy. I have made you worthy. Even with all of the training in the world, you are not qualified without Me. You can't earn My anointing. I'm the one who gives it to you.*

As I continued to pray that morning, I felt a weight released from my heart. The pressure was off. My stress was gone. The guilt vanished. Instead of beating myself up, I enjoyed a sweet and Spirit-filled time with God. God helped me see that I don't have to earn His mercy, His grace, His anointing, and most important, His love.

You know what else? The conference was awesome. God did many wonderful and amazing things. As we closed our time together, every single woman in that room made a commitment to be willing to serve.

I believe God wants us to stop trying to earn His love and forgiveness. Instead, we need to start receiving what He has already done so we can enjoy spending time with Him. God wants His love for you to be your motivation in life.

Where Do I Start?
When you feel loved by God, it comes out in practical ways. Let's say you're applying for a job you really want and feel nervous and anxious. Right before the interview, take a few minutes to call to mind how much God loves and values you. Soak in His presence and let Him remind you of your worth. Remember the words of Jesus, "What is the price of two sparrows—one copper coin? But not a single sparrow can fall to the ground without

your Father knowing it. And the very hairs on your head are all numbered. So don't be afraid; you are more valuable to God than a whole flock of sparrows" (Matthew 10:29-31). Then walk into that interview confident and expectant.

This is also good preparation before you are about to volunteer or lead an outreach. Take some time meditating in the presence of God and allow Him to show His love to you. I guarantee your love tank will be full and you'll be motivated to serve others wholeheartedly and share His love with them.

David wrote in Psalm 59:16, "Each morning I will sing with joy about [God's] unfailing love." I challenge you to begin every day by allowing God to love on you and fill you up. This isn't a one-time deal. There will be days you will need to run to God several times to get refilled with His love. Keep at it.

Close to God's Heart

David was a great leader who followed after God's own heart. But he was also human and had his share of foibles and failures. In his psalms he constantly remarks on knowing God's love for him. "I am *always aware* of your unfailing love, and I have lived according to your truth" (Psalm 26:3, emphasis added).

We can learn so much from studying David's life. His devotion to God is a powerful illustration of how to live in awareness of God's unfailing and personal love for you. David's motivation and willingness came from a pure desire to represent God and give Him the glory. It began publically when he faced Goliath, who was mocking God. I love David's response:

You come to me with sword, spear, and javelin, but
I come to you in the name of the LORD of Heaven's
Armies—the God of the armies of Israel, whom you

have defied. Today the LORD will conquer you, and I will kill you and cut off your head. And then I will give the dead bodies of your men to the birds and wild animals, and the whole world will know that there is a God in Israel! And everyone assembled here will know that the LORD rescues his people, but not with sword and spear. This is the LORD's battle, and he will give you to us!

1 SAMUEL 17:45-47

Whenever I read David's psalms, I cross-reference them to 1 and 2 Samuel so I can better understand what was actually happening in his life at the time he was writing them. Some of the most beautiful and uplifting passages were penned when he was in the midst of seemingly hopeless situations.

Alone, Discouraged . . . and Loved

Though he was anointed as king when he was just a shepherd boy, David didn't immediately ascend to the throne to replace King Saul. Saul was jealous of his successor, threatened by the young man's growing popularity and accomplishments as a military leader. The king was determined to eliminate the threat to his crown, so he put a contract out on David's life.

Once David learned of Saul's plan, his life changed dramatically: he became a man on the run. When David wrote Psalm 63, he was exiled in the wilderness, far from the comforts and familiarity of home. He wasn't abandoned because of his own wrongdoing. His hopeless situation was through no fault of his own.

If you were David, how would you have felt? Would you think that God had abandoned you? Would you question your purpose in life?

I believe one of the reasons David was successful is because his loving attitude toward God never faltered. Rather than spiraling down in misery, he wrote a love song to God. I love his words:

O God, you are my God;
    I earnestly search for you.
My soul thirsts for you;
    my whole body longs for you
in this parched and weary land
    where there is no water.
I have seen you in your sanctuary
    and gazed upon your power and glory.
Your unfailing love is better than life itself;
    how I praise you!
I will praise you as long as I live,
    lifting up my hands to you in prayer.
You satisfy me more than the richest feast.
    I will praise you with songs of joy.

I lie awake thinking of you,
    meditating on you through the night.
PSALM 63:1-6

You can sense David's sincere longing for God. His words aren't merely lip service.

Is this how you would describe the way God's love makes you feel? Are His love and your relationship with Him better than life? If you were stripped of money, possessions, job security, talents, smarts, beauty, and even loved ones—essentially all that you have—would God be more than enough for you?

If not, press into Him. Allow God to embrace you with the magnitude of His love. He wants you to know at the deepest level of your soul that His love is more than enough.

As you read this, perhaps you feel alone. Maybe you struggle with being abandoned, left out, or disregarded. You may feel alone even in a crowded room. You may live with your family but still feel miles apart, believing no one knows what you're going through. Guess what? God does. And He never intended for you to live this life on your own in your own strength. With Him you are never alone. With Him you can do all things. With Him, you can feel loved, not lost or forsaken.

God knows your troubles. He knows your mistakes. He knows your best efforts. He knows your failed attempts. And none of it changes how much He loves you. "Neither death nor life, neither angels nor demons, neither the present nor the future, nor any powers, neither height nor depth, nor anything else in all creation, will be able to separate us from the love of God that is in Christ Jesus our Lord" (Romans 8:38-39, NIV). In your own wilderness, when you acknowledge with your heart and your head that God loves you, you can find joy and purpose in any circumstance.

Though it hasn't always been easy, Leisa has allowed herself to be enveloped by God's love.

Before coming to the Dream Center in 2008, I went through a devastating divorce. I was so distraught I tried to kill myself. After arriving on campus and entering the discipleship program, I knew God loved me but I still felt alone and discouraged. Four years later, I'm still serving and giving back to the ministry that gave so much to me. Through this process I have learned about

God's love and that though problems may come, He will always be there for me. When I have felt overwhelmed, I make the choice to draw closer to Him and let Him love on me.

God's Enduring Love

I've learned that even in the face of tragedy, we can still experience God's love. In these moments, we have the opportunity to trust Him or doubt His goodness and love. The choice is up to us.

When Matthew and I had been married for two years, the mommy bug bit me. I desperately wanted a child. We tried to conceive for an entire year, each month a hopeful disappointment. One day when I was feeling particularly upset, I remembered the words of the sweet and very candid Filipino ladies at some of my food truck sites: "If you keep lifting so many heavy boxes, you'll never be able to have kids!" I assumed it was an old wives' tale, so I would smile and nod politely, but keep on working. But a year later, I feared there was some truth to what they had said.

Then I got pregnant. When Matthew and I saw the plus sign on the pregnancy test, we were elated. Immediately, we drove to my parents' house to share the good news. As a first-time mom, I couldn't contain my excitement and had a permanent smile on my face. I wanted to tell everyone the good news, but Matthew and I decided to wait until after the first trimester. Around the twelfth week, we made the big announcement to the church. Everyone shared in our delight.

A few days later, I went to the doctor's office for a second ultrasound. Matthew and I had just become first-time homeowners and moving day was the same day as my appointment. Matthew needed to be on hand at our new condominium. I missed him and wished he was by my side, but I knew Matthew was with me in spirit.

I nervously lay on the examining table as the doctor poured the cool gel on my stomach and swiftly moved the handheld scanner over my stomach. My eyes fixed on the ultrasound machine's screen, my ears listening for the distinct whooshing sound and the rhythmic thump of my baby's heartbeat. But I didn't hear anything except static.

I shot a glance at my doctor. She was looking at the screen, too, but had a stoic expression. Still, I couldn't help but notice a glint of worry in her eyes. Calmly, she put the scanner down and told me to get dressed and come to her office. It was obvious that something was wrong.

When I stood up and my bare feet touched the floor, a chill went through my body. My hands shook as I fumbled for my clothes. Though I knew there was a problem, I wasn't prepared for what she was about to tell me.

I was quiet when I sat down in her office. The doctor folded her hands on the desk and explained that I would miscarry in a few days.

I wanted to get out of there fast, before the flood of tears began. As the doctor continued telling me what to expect, I nodded numbly. *Maybe this is a dream. A really bad dream. Maybe if I close my eyes I'll wake up and this nightmare will be over.*

By the time I got to my car, I was sobbing relentlessly. It's a wonder I could see to drive home safely. When I told Matthew what the doctor said, he held me in his arms and we cried together.

When I started bleeding a few nights later, I continued to deny the truth of what was happening. Matthew comforted me as best he could. Hoping for God to perform a miracle,

I headed out the next morning to work on my food truck site. By the end of the day, I started having contractions, which shocked me. The doctor hadn't given me any specifics of what happens during a miscarriage. I was in severe pain, physically and emotionally. My heart broke a little more with each cramp. Matthew was at church, studying and preparing for Sunday's message. I knew it wouldn't be good for me to be alone, so I headed to my parents' house.

I prayed as I drove, spitting out a few words in between my uncontrollable sobbing. "Is this it, God?" I voiced with a mixture of sadness and doubt. "Will I ever have a baby?"

I desperately grasped for hope. I recited Psalm 37:4, "Delight yourself in the LORD, and he will give you the desires of your heart" (NIV). My heart's desire was to have a baby, and I believed God would not go back on His promise.

The actual miscarriage was a long and painful experience, but I was grateful for my parents' emotional support. I let Matthew know where I was and what was happening and he offered to come over immediately, but I assured him I was in good hands. I stayed in my parents' bedroom all day, with my mom checking on me periodically. I really did want to be alone. I went back home late that night, and after Matthew finally arrived home, we grieved and cried together.

The following week, I had a D and C at an outpatient facility while Matthew anxiously waited and prayed for me in the lobby. The pain medication they gave me did its job—it was good not to feel.

For weeks after, I was beset by feelings of devastation. Though my heart was breaking, Matthew's unfailing support helped me get through as we grieved the loss together. He comments on this unforgettable experience:

The miscarriage hit both of us hard, but I was amazed at the strength Caroline showed in getting back up. I couldn't find the perfect words to comfort her. But I didn't have to. We both needed to be near each other. She just needed someone to support her. In time, her amazing strength returned.

Though the emotional pain eased up after that point, I had no compelling desire to try to conceive again. I needed to heal from the experience. During this time of great sorrow, Psalm 34:18 came alive in my heart—"The LORD is close to the broken-hearted; he rescues those whose spirits are crushed." Though I wasn't sure what the future would hold, God was faithful in being present. Over time, true to His Word, I felt Him close by, even as my heart unraveled within.

A year later, I knew I was ready to try again, though I was still apprehensive. My anxiety hadn't completely subsided, but I made the choice to uphold my faith. Nine months later, Matthew and I welcomed beautiful Mia into the world. Two and a half years later, Caden, our handsome rascal, arrived. God's love is faithful and "endures through every circumstance" (1 Corinthians 13:7). He will not fail you when you stand firm in His love, no matter what you are going through.

Matthew learned his own lessons during this time:

Losing our child was heartbreaking. One day we were preparing the baby's room, eagerly awaiting the day we would be bringing our first child home, and the next moment we were facing the harsh reality that it wasn't going to happen. At first, I wept and wanted to die. Then, like King David when he lost his child, I thought, *What is done is done. It's time to move on.*

This kind of heartbreak changes your ministry in many ways. Every season of brokenness makes you stronger. People have said that we are defined by our victories. I believe that we are defined by how we respond to loss. I realized that this moment of brokenness would one day become a divine weapon of usefulness for Him.

The Power of God's Love

I'm inspired by Danielle, who works at the Dream Center. Though she has experienced tragedy, she has made the commitment to live her life and serve others, motivated by the love of God. She constantly speaks of how powerful God's love is, evidenced by her story:

> I was born into a military family. My father's life was the United States Marine Corps, and he was rarely around. When I was seven years old, my parents divorced. My mother remarried in June of 2003. Little did I know that less than six months later my life would be radically altered.
>
> On October 16, 2003, my sister and I witnessed our mother murder our stepfather. I was forced to move in with my father, who I barely knew.
>
> Six months later in April 2004, I received Christ and became a member of a local youth group. My mother was convicted of murder and sentenced to twenty-eight years in prison. During a retrial, I was coerced into testifying against my mother. She received a life sentence without parole and a $100,000 fine.

I became lost, guilt ridden, and ashamed. I was so angry and full of hatred. I built up walls around my heart and hurt those around me before they had a chance to hurt me. Though I had many leaders ministering into my life and telling me God was with me, I just couldn't feel Him.

After my mother had been in prison for six years, I decided to visit her and face the music. After what felt like an eternity of silence, she said, "Danielle, I got saved in April of 2004, and I have been living my life for God ever since." I left the prison skeptical of the change in her life.

A few months later I visited her again. The emptiness that I was used to seeing in her eyes had been replaced with love, remorse, and hope. She leaned over the table and said to me, "I am so sorry for everything I put you through. I want you to know that I love you and I realize I can't make it up to you on the outside. I know that God's plan for my life is to help women who don't have anything to live for on the inside."

On the long walk back to my car I asked God, "Is Mom's change genuine?" God sweetly whispered to me, *She is My child just as you are My child. I am changing her life just as I am changing yours. She is going to move mountains on the inside. You are going to move mountains on the outside.* At that moment I felt a shower of God's love and grace pour over me. I felt like I could conquer the world. And then He spoke 2 Timothy 1:7 into my heart: "God has not given us a spirit of fear and timidity, but of power, love, and self-discipline." Nothing I had been through was in vain, but was going to be an answer to many prayers in the future. I began to speak life into people and help them tap into God's potential for them.

When I first walked into the Los Angeles Dream Center, I felt God say, *Welcome home.*

In my life, I have learned two key principles. First, God did not create me to do this life alone. Every person I encounter has something that I can learn from them. It is my responsibility to tap into the hidden treasures that God has so carefully and meticulously designed for me.

Second, I have learned to love people where they are, instead of where they are supposed to be. If God can take a woman with a mental disorder who lacks the ability to feel emotion and transform her into His vessel in a maximum-security prison, why can't we choose to release our finite perspective and embrace God's higher perspective of those around us? I have chosen to break the social norm and accept my mother as the child of God He created rather than define her as the murderer that the world knows her to be. I am proud to be her daughter.

God is the God of hope, restoration, and new beginnings. The evidence of God's faithfulness is written all over my life. Outsiders look at my life as a terrible tragedy, but I choose to see it as a beautiful love letter God has handcrafted for me to share with the world.

Danielle allowed God's love to fill her and give her the strength and courage to respond to her circumstances. Her bright outlook on her life and future is a strong reminder that God's love is able to overcome even the most difficult situations. Her heart for others reflects the love, grace, and mercy God has lavished on her.

Responding Supernaturally in Love

When David was running for his life from King Saul, he often hid out in caves. On one occasion, a group of men joined him. This ragtag bunch would become the men God used to defend David—"men who were in trouble or in debt or who were just discontented" (1 Samuel 22:2). Sounds like many of us at the Dream Center whom God is using to accomplish His mission!

In 1 Samuel 24, King Saul takes three thousand of his best-trained men to hunt down David and his men. When the king stopped at one point to relieve himself, he chose the very cave where David and his men were concealed. David's golden opportunity had come! He could take down his enemy, fully justified in the attack.

> "Now's your opportunity!" David's men whispered to him. "Today the LORD is telling you, 'I will certainly put your enemy into your power, to do with as you wish.'" So David crept forward and cut off a piece of the hem of Saul's robe.
>
> But then David's conscience began bothering him because he had cut Saul's robe. "The LORD knows I shouldn't have done that to my lord the king," he said to his men. "The LORD forbid that I should do this to my lord the king and attack the LORD's anointed one, for the LORD himself has chosen him." So David restrained his men and did not let them kill Saul.
>
> I SAMUEL 24:4-7

David supernaturally approached this situation with God's love, the same perspective that fills Psalm 57. "I look to you for protection. I will hide beneath the shadow of your wings until the danger passes by. I cry out to God Most High, to God who will fulfill his purpose for me. He will send help from heaven to rescue me, disgracing those who hound me. My God will send forth his *unfailing love* and faithfulness" (verses 1-3, emphasis added).

That same unfailing love and faithfulness are available to you. You may be in a very difficult situation that looks impossible. I challenge you not to respond in brokenness. Respond in love and make decisions out of wholeness.

Don't cut ties with family because you have been hurt by them. Before making such a critical decision, let God love on you and then see if your perspective is the same. Don't quit your job because the promotion you wanted was given to someone else. Let God love on you and then wait for His guidance. Don't stop volunteering because you feel underappreciated. Let God love on you and remind you that you are living your life and serving others for Him, that He sees it all, and that He will reward you for all.

Fallen, But Loved

What happens when we fail? When we miss the mark? When we sin? Is it possible to approach our mistakes with God's love?

David, now king, was devoted to God, worshiping and praising Him daily. But David wasn't perfect. Despite his deep commitment and faithfulness to God, he found himself in deep sin—a triumvirate of adultery, lies, and murder. Honestly, I'm surprised that David, a handsome and powerful leader, didn't fall into sin more often. But how tragic when he did.

Second Samuel 11 details King David's plunge down a slippery slope of sinful behavior. I think he basically broke every one of the Ten Commandments in one shot. David lusted after Bathsheba, a married woman, and they had a steamy affair.

Bathsheba became pregnant and David began damage control. He schemed his cover-up carefully. Bathsheba's husband, Uriah, was away at battle, so David had Uriah sent home, ostensibly to give a battle report, but with the suggestion that he enjoy time with his wife. A loyal soldier, Uriah came home to report but did not spend the night with his wife; his duty was to fight beside his comrades. David then sent Uriah to the front lines and he died, loyal to his king to the end.

David thought he was now in the clear, that he and Bathsheba could marry and live happily ever after. But the prophet Nathan called David out on his sin, leading to confession and repentance. Psalm 51 pictures David at one of the lowest points in his life. But overcome with grief and shame, he still knew that God loved him.

> Have mercy on me, O God,
>   because of your *unfailing love.*
> Because of your great compassion,
>   blot out the stain of my sins.
> Wash me clean from my guilt.
>   Purify me from my sin.
> PSALM 51:1-2 (EMPHASIS ADDED)

You may have fallen from grace. Maybe there are areas in your life you know you need to change. Perhaps you are not living right. Even on our best days, we sin and feel unworthy of God's great and perfect love. Sin keeps us from God. Most times it makes us afraid to come to Him, even if we're genuinely sorry. It feels almost impossible when we are so ashamed.

Don't wait. Don't hesitate to come to God and confess your failures. Pray for forgiveness. Ask Him for strength to overcome the things that hold you back from experiencing His great gift of love.

If you want to enjoy the journey of life and the adventure of serving others, you have to believe with all your heart that God loves you in a personal way. Make His love your motivator. Let it compel you to do the right thing in all circumstances, even if it seems impossible in your human power. Draw upon the power of God's love to live fully and abundantly.

CHAPTER 9

OUR WANTS VS. GOD'S WANTS

God is working in you, giving you the desire
and the power to do what pleases him.

—— PHILIPPIANS 2:13 ——

OVER THE YEARS I've noticed a common thread among people who are hesitant or stuck about serving others. They assume God's plan for them will be something they will hate, it will drastically interfere with their own lives or plans, or it will require an unreasonable amount of time or money.

Let me set the record straight. God wants you to have purpose and feel fulfilled. If you find yourself questioning His plans for your life, relax and let Him direct you. If you trust Him, you will find that your plans and His plans match up better than you expected. Instead of fighting against your ideas of what God desires of you, get on board with Him.

Seventeen years ago, Phyllis did just that. Though God called her to the Dream Center, it took her a while to get there. At first she outright refused to attend our church, let alone serve, because it was located in a dangerous, low-income area. But after several weeks, unable to avoid the gnawing in her spirit to obey, she finally came to a Thursday night service.

Today, Phyllis couldn't imagine doing anything different.

"It's a pleasure to serve. It's wonderful to see the buses go out and pick up people, especially children, and hear what the Lord has done in their lives. His blessings are overwhelming. I feel very honored to be a part of this wonderful ministry and vision."

Do you want all that God has made available to you? Do you want to take Him up on all His promises? Do you want to enjoy a journey with Him instead of walking it alone? Do you want to walk on water? Well, guess what? God wants these very things for you too!

The apostle Paul encourages followers of Christ, "Work hard so you can present yourself to God and receive his approval," adding this comparison: "Expensive utensils are used for special occasions, and the cheap ones are for everyday use. If you keep yourself pure, you will be a special utensil for honorable use. Your life will be clean, and you will be ready for the Master to use you for every good work" (2 Timothy 2:15, 20-21).

Do you want to be honorably used by God? I believe that most people do. And God wants to use us. He can use anybody, wherever you are, whatever you are doing, whether it's in "ministry" or not. You don't have to be a missionary, work at the Dream Center, or lead outreaches at your church. One day we will stand before God, knowing that we accomplished what He made us to do and became who He wanted us to be.

The passage of Scripture in 2 Timothy gives us a condition to be used for "honorable use." We are called to keep ourselves pure. The first thought that comes to mind when I read this is living without sin.

Romans 6 tells us, "Don't you realize that you become the slave of whatever you choose to obey? You can be a slave to sin, which leads to death, or you can choose to obey God, which leads to righteous living. . . . When you were slaves to sin, you were free from the obligation to do right. And what was the result? You are now ashamed of the things you used to do, things that end in eternal doom. But now you are free from the power of sin and have become slaves of God. Now you do those things that lead to holiness and result in eternal life" (verses 16, 20-22). Do you want to be a slave to something that hurts you or makes you feel ashamed? Of course not! God doesn't want you to either.

Sin or a Bad Choice?

The word *sin* makes a lot of people feel uncomfortable. Some people believe everything that's fun is a sin. Other people feel there is no such thing as sin because God is love and we are not bound by restrictions or consequences for the way we live.

This reminds me of a debate that started between Matthew and me eight years ago. For most of my life, I had lived with symptoms of a cold that never went away. It was particularly bad during the first three years I lived at the Dream Center. I was always congested, and my nose was always raw.

Then I came across a book on health that explained the harmful effects of eating pork and shellfish. So I decided to eliminate pork and shellfish from my diet. After two months, I stopped being sick and wasn't congested anymore. Now, I don't believe it was a sin for me to eat those things. I certainly wasn't defiling my spirit or going to hell for eating pork lo mein or shrimp cocktail. It just happened that refraining from those foods was better for my health.

I was so excited that I tried to convince Matthew to give up those foods. At first my efforts to change his eating habits made him want them even more. When we'd go out to eat, it seemed like he ordered bacon at every meal. Matthew playfully accused me of judging these foods as sin. Eventually I gave up my crusade to reform Matthew's diet but kept the reforms for my own.

There are certain things we shouldn't do—not because they're necessarily sins, but because they will harm us physically, emotionally, mentally, or even spiritually.

Here's another illustration: For years, every night when I got in bed I asked God to forgive me for not spending more time in His Word and in prayer. My entire prayer time was spent beating myself up instead of using that time to connect with Him. I was in a constant cycle of shame and guilt because I was so hung up on how much time was enough. Did I have to pray a half hour a day? An hour? Did I have to set aside blocks of time several times a day? In the morning? Or at night? Or both?

I finally felt God impress on my heart that His love, His grace, and His approval did not depend on anything I could do. Developing my relationship with God isn't a sin issue. It's a heart issue. Of course we have to regularly spend time with God. How else are we going to live out our faith walk? But I had to stop focusing so much on how or when I did it. I had to connect with God because I wanted to. Not because He would be mad or disappointed if I didn't.

And why wouldn't I want to spend time in prayer seeking guidance, direction, and wisdom from an all-knowing God who loves me unconditionally? Who knows my future and what will keep me excited about living this life? Why wouldn't I want to study God's truths about life, business, and relationships when He orchestrated this whole world and put its laws in motion? Not spending regular time with God isn't necessarily a sin, but it will keep you from experiencing His power, joy, and peace in your life.

The Business of Being Pure

So what is sin? There are specific sins mentioned in the Bible, but if you have questions, I would advise talking it over with your pastor or spiritual leader as well as listening to the prompting of the Holy Spirit as a guide and help.

As a helpful guideline, I like this teaching from the apostle Paul: "You say, 'I am allowed to do anything'—but not everything is good for you. You say, 'I am allowed to do anything'—but not everything is beneficial" (1 Corinthians 10:23). It's certainly not a sin to eat, for instance, but food can become an idol in our lives. Anything that interferes with our relationship with God is a sin. He wants us to run from sin so we can live the abundant and free life He intended us to have.

Sin is just as much about the do's as it is about the don'ts. I know some Christians who feel they are pure, blameless, and whole because they don't do anything wrong. That mind-set could easily lead to pride and a feeling of being better than others. A pure life is lived humbly, knowing every moment that you need God.

Jesus tells the story of two people who held differing definitions of sin:

> Two men went to the Temple to pray. One was a
> Pharisee, and the other was a despised tax collector.
> The Pharisee stood by himself and prayed this prayer:
> "I thank you, God, that I am not a sinner like everyone
> else. For I don't cheat, I don't sin, and I don't commit
> adultery. I'm certainly not like that tax collector! I fast
> twice a week, and I give you a tenth of my income."
> But the tax collector stood at a distance and dared
> not even lift his eyes to heaven as he prayed. Instead, he

beat his chest in sorrow, saying, "O God, be merciful to me, for I am a sinner." I tell you, this sinner, not the Pharisee, returned home justified before God. For those who exalt themselves will be humbled, and those who humble themselves will be exalted.

LUKE 18:10-14

Living a pure life isn't about being perfect. It's about setting ourselves apart from this world and living for Jesus, not for others. It's about looking to Him to guide our ambitions and our motivations. It's about knowing we are made pure through His sacrifice, not our good works.

Living a pure life also means affirming certain promises from God. First, we'll never be tempted beyond our ability to withstand, and when we are tempted He will provide us a way out (1 Corinthians 10:13). Second, when we are weak and struggling, we are made strong through Christ (2 Corinthians 12:9-10).

How Much Is Enough?

When it comes to living a life of purity and following the call to serve others, I know that many people struggle with determining how much time or money they need to give in service. It's easy to stumble our way through life feeling guilty because we think we're not doing enough.

Though my friend Shelly initially struggled with not having a lot of time to serve, she came to realize that she just had to be obedient in what she had to offer. God would take care of the rest.

I came to the Dream Center five years ago. My husband and I own an advertising agency, and we spend most of our time traveling for business. The only day of the week I had available to serve was Tuesday afternoon. So from 1 to 4 p.m., I hit the streets in a beat-up truck filled with food.

I talked to single moms working three jobs, drug dealers, gang members, and kids who had never met their dads. I saw so much pain, loss, and emptiness. Week after week, I couldn't wait for Tuesdays to come because I knew I had the hope these people needed—Jesus.

I agonized over the limited time that I had to serve. At the end of each Tuesday, I would drive home exhilarated from being able to help others but also sick to my stomach that I couldn't do more. I knew because of my work schedule, I couldn't expand my time at the Dream Center, so I begged God for more opportunities to serve. It's funny how God loves to answer those kinds of prayers.

Walking around the Dream Center campus one day, I noticed a group of teenage girls wearing black T-shirts. I found out that they were part of a life transformation program called Discipleship and lived on campus full-time. I learned more about their program and felt this was the opportunity God had opened up. I began working with the girls on Tuesdays after my food truck shift was done.

In the process of serving others, I recognized that I am the church, part of the body of Christ. Serving is a 24/7 job, not something that you do just one day or seven days a week. I am a representative for Jesus every minute of every day. Opportunities to serve are everywhere. You just need to follow God's voice. And if He gives you a desire to do something, He will find a way to make it happen.

God says He blesses in proportion to our giving. "Give, and you will receive. Your gift will return to you in full—pressed down, shaken together to make room for more, running over, and poured into your lap. The amount you give will determine the amount you get back" (Luke 6:38).

How much do you have to give above your tithe? Well, how much do you *want* to give? God is not looking for a specific time or monetary sacrifice. He's just looking for our willingness to help others. The particulars are up to us.

It's motivating to serve. When we care and provide for God's children, we experience unimaginable joy, the fullness of His love, and His grace in action. We enjoy His blessings so we can continue to bless others and further His Kingdom.

Our View of God

It's important to approach our service with the right perception of God. He is not a stern taskmaster who forces us to follow His call. He doesn't want us to cower in our faith, afraid to take risks or use our talents and gifts to serve Him. He is not keeping score of how much time we invest in furthering His Kingdom, ready to break us down if it's not enough.

My perception of God has changed over the last ten years. Initially, my vision and understanding of Him was limited. I expect ten years from now, with even more life experience and knowledge, I'll understand God a lot more deeply than I do today.

Because I spent years being afraid of God, it made me fearful to take risks. But the more I grew in my relationship with Him, praying and studying His Word, the more I understood how wrong my thinking was. God isn't demanding or impossible to please. He is loving, kind, merciful, and full of grace. And He has good plans and desires for us.

Taskmaster or Father?

In Matthew 25 Jesus tells the parable of the talents, a good illustration of how I used to view God. In this story, a man entrusts three of his servants with different amounts of money as he leaves on a trip. One man receives five talents, another two, and the last, one. In the master's absence, his servants are to be responsible for their stewardship of what they have received.

These men have the same master but have different perceptions of him. The man with the five talents is not afraid of the responsibility, nor is he intimidated by how successful, powerful, and blessed his master is. He's willing to take a risk and invests the funds, ultimately doubling his master's money. The second servant takes the same leap of faith and also doubles the money.

The third servant is nervous. He has some false notions about his master. Mostly, the servant fears him. I understand this man's hesitance. Growing up, I always assumed God was mad at me. I desperately wanted to please Him, but never thought I did. I always seemed to come up short and was convinced God was constantly disappointed in me.

The man with the one talent is afraid of trying and failing, so he shirks his responsibility. He buries the money. When the master returns and questions the status of his investment, the third man responds, "I knew you were a harsh man, harvesting crops you didn't plant and gathering crops you didn't cultivate. I was afraid I would lose your money, so I hid it in the earth. Look, here is your money back" (Matthew 25:24-25).

The master chews him out. "You wicked and lazy servant! If you knew I harvested crops I didn't plant and gathered crops I didn't cultivate, why didn't you deposit my money in the bank? At least I could have gotten some interest on it" (Matthew 25:26-27). Ouch!

The master in this parable represents God. The servant who hid his talent approached his task with the wrong view of his master. He was led by fear. He didn't know it was acceptable to take risks and use his talents to turn a profit. He was too scared to even try.

I know that fear of stepping out into the great unknown. But I also know the freedom you can experience when you come to a true understanding of the character of God.

A distorted image of God will hold us back from doing what He has called us to do. But when we see God as a loving Father who wants the best for us, we will want nothing more than to obey Him—not out of fear, but out of love. Once my views changed, I was able to serve God and others from a willing spirit.

God is not keeping track of how many hours you devote to providing for the needs of others. All I know for certain is that the more you get to know God and the more your faith grows, the more you will want to serve.

Give of yourself not because you are afraid that God will be mad if you don't. Give out of a willing heart. Give because injustice breaks your heart. Give because seeing others suffer moves you to do something about it.

Not on Our Own

We can't live a pure life without God's help. I love that God asks us to live right and to step out in faith for Him but doesn't expect or ask us to do it on our own. The Holy Spirit will be beside us. "We have received God's Spirit (not the world's spirit), so we can know the wonderful things God has freely given us" (1 Corinthians 2:12).

Right before Matthew and I sold our last house, I went through every room and made a list of what we needed to fix.

My husband is gifted in many areas, but he is not a handyman. So I asked a few of his handier assistants to help me go through the to-do list. Robert Moore was one of the guys who came over that day.

Robert is a graduate of our discipleship program. He grew up in a gang in South Central Los Angeles and spent over twenty years in prison. Tall, with broad shoulders and bulging muscles, Robert looks intimidating. But he's really just a big teddy bear with a great smile.

Number one on the list was to replace the mirrored sliding doors on my son's closet. I had had problems with those doors since the day we moved in. Our first hurdle was that the replacement door frames were too long for the opening. Robert was confident he could fix it. "All I need is a hacksaw," he said enthusiastically. I didn't even know what a hacksaw was. Robert knocked on our neighbor's door and asked if he could borrow a hacksaw. Lord only knows what they were thinking! He fixed the closet in under an hour.

From there, we moved outside to clear away a huge woodpile on the side of the house. It had been there for years and was an eyesore. As all of us helped load the wood onto a truck, a huge rat jumped out from the pile and started jumping around like a fish out of water. We all screamed. Except Robert. In a split second, he picked up a piece of wood and chucked it at the rat. Bull's-eye! It happened so fast that at first I was in shock, but then I burst out laughing.

There wasn't anything that Robert couldn't do, and I was in awe of his skills. We finished everything on the list that day because of Robert. He had the skills, experience, and strength I lacked. He saved us a lot of money and time, and without him I wouldn't have been able to get our house ready to be sold.

The Great Helper

Let me be clear: I'm not comparing the Holy Spirit to a handy-man. Yet I wouldn't be able to live right or do the things God has called me to do without the Holy Spirit. He gives me the skills I need to mature in my faith and serve others.

The apostle Paul taught how being led by the Spirit produces His fruit in us:

> Let the Holy Spirit guide your lives. Then you won't be doing what your sinful nature craves. The sinful nature wants to do evil, which is just the opposite of what the Spirit wants. And the Spirit gives us desires that are the opposite of what the sinful nature desires. These two forces are constantly fighting each other, so you are not free to carry out your good intentions. But when you are directed by the Spirit, you are not under obligation to the law of Moses. . . .
>
> The Holy Spirit produces this kind of fruit in our lives: *love, joy, peace, patience, kindness, goodness, faithfulness, gentleness, and self-control.* There is no law against these things!
>
> GALATIANS 5:16-18, 22-23 (EMPHASIS ADDED)

Growing up, I believed the fruits of the Spirit were qualities I had to work hard to achieve, but as I matured in my faith I realized that it's not my job to strive for them. It's only my job to allow my life to be controlled by the Holy Spirit. Only then will I naturally produce these fruits.

Start Living by the Spirit

Why try to do what God is asking you to do without His help? Why make your life so much harder than it has to be when you have the best possible resource, who is available all the time, to guide you?

The Holy Spirit will help you be what you need to be and get done what you need to get done. He will help you discern what is right and wrong; when it is time to give or to withhold; when it is time to sell or to buy; when it is time to expand your business or when it is time to maintain the status quo for a season. The Holy Spirit has your best interest in mind and wants you to enjoy immeasurable success.

Oftentimes I have found that God knows what I want more than I do, and it takes stepping out in faith to discover that. Remember how I cringed at the thought of serving in Los Angeles? "Anywhere but here, God," I prayed. But God knew this is where I belonged. Today I love the city and can't imagine serving or living anywhere else. When you step out in faith and trust the Holy Spirit to guide you, you will find new dreams and new desires for others that you didn't even know were inside of you.

God is on your side. He wants you to accomplish more than you could ever imagine. He wants your life to be an exciting adventure. He wants to reveal His supernatural power through you. When you faithfully serve others and make a difference, you'll never have to worry about whether or not your desires are God's. They already are!

PART III

DOING

Prayer in action is love, and love in action is service. Try to give unconditionally whatever a person needs in the moment. The point is to do something, however small, and show you care through your actions by giving your time. . . . We are all God's children so it is important to share His gifts. Do not worry about why problems exist in the world—just respond to people's needs. . . . We feel what we are doing is just a drop in the ocean, but that ocean would be less without that drop.

MOTHER TERESA

CHAPTER 10

THE *YOU* IN SERVING

Remove the heavy yoke of oppression. . . . Feed the hungry,
and help those in trouble. Then your light will shine out from
the darkness, and the darkness around you will be as bright as noon.
The LORD will guide you continually, giving you water
when you are dry and restoring your strength.

—— ISAIAH 58:9-11 ——

I MEET MANY PEOPLE who feel hopelessly stuck. They struggle with the same issues, problems, and attitudes for years. Many refuse to learn from their mistakes and ultimately wallow in regret their whole lives.

I'm not talking about people who come to the Dream Center for help. I'm talking about Christians who have been in church all their lives yet who are not living the life of freedom and abundance that Jesus came to give.

I once had a conversation with a woman in her sixties. She told me her troubled life story and then listed all the reasons she hadn't lived the kind of good life she wanted. She grew up poor and had to support her family by cleaning houses.

Initially, I felt sorry for her and could understand her current attitude, given her particular setbacks and challenges. Despite her excuses, I could see that she loved God. But I could also see how the excuses held her back from living out God's promises.

This woman had all the tools she needed to change her life. She had a personal relationship with God. She read the Bible and powerful Christian books. She knew about God's promises of victory, strength, and provision. My compassion turned to pity. This woman was living a less-than kind of life based on excuses, not legitimate reasons. She never took God at His Word. She never applied biblical principles to her life. She never stood on His promises.

I know she's not alone. A lot of believers are paralyzed by brokenness. It seems impossible to change or break free from shackles like addiction, unforgiveness, and regret.

Serving Others Is Self-Help

Some people strive for a better life but still seem stuck. They may even own a dozen self-help books to help "fix" them. There is a countless supply of books you can buy that claim to have the answer on how to be confident, successful, happy, and fulfilled—how to live purposefully, have a great marriage, live with gratitude, and so on. It seems every day a new book is released on how we can improve, be healed from emotional trauma, or become whole in some way. I'm not against self-help books by any means, but . . . it makes me wonder.

As I've said, there are 358 references in the Bible to helping the poor, the needy, the widow, and the orphan. Could it be that the reason we still need to buy these self-help books is because we are not helping others and doing what God has asked us to do over three hundred times?

When we obey God and serve others, He changes us from the inside out. He shapes our hearts to better reflect His. We can even experience healing. I find we are always at our best when we are serving.

Making the Broken Whole

When I think how helping others heals the one who is serving,
I think of Becky. For the last four years she has been involved
in Project Prevention, making weekly visits to families, coordi-
nating sixty volunteers per week, and delivering furniture and
other essentials. You would never know that she had endured
an extremely hard life. Becky says,

> I was placed into the foster-care system immediately
> after birth. I was on a heart monitor due to severe sleep
> apnea. My birth mother had been on seizure medication
> during her pregnancy, which had compromised me in
> the womb. I was on a monitor for over a year and was
> inconsolable when I cried. When I was three I became
> very ill and was hospitalized for two weeks. I had sixteen
> inches of dead intestines removed.
>
> After five years of court hearings, I was finally
> adopted by my foster parents. Over the course of thirty
> years, my parents have fostered hundreds of children,
> most of them with major health issues. Most of my
> brothers and sisters and I had to grow up very fast.
> We had to learn how to handle babies and children
> who were on heart monitors or trachea machines, had
> Down syndrome, were addicted to drugs in utero, had
> been sexually abused, and so on. As a child, I never
> understood why I couldn't have been raised in a normal
> family.
>
> I followed in my older brothers' footsteps of party-
> ing and drinking. I got pregnant at nineteen and was
> planning on having an abortion. When I went in for the
> abortion, the doctor couldn't find the baby. Four hours

later, my right fallopian tube had ruptured and I started bleeding internally. I needed emergency surgery.

For three years, I lived with an abusive boyfriend. I started drinking, which magnified my bad temper. Finally, one of my brothers came and took me out of that situation. My drinking got worse.

When I was twenty-two, I moved three hours from home and had my first encounter with God. I decided to stop partying so much and start attending church. I found out about the Dream Center and heard about their outreaches.

A fire ignited inside me—more than anything else, I wanted to help children who couldn't help themselves. I had spent so many years of my youth despising the kids I was raised with and the life I was given. In that moment I fell to my knees and started crying.

When I first arrived at the Dream Center, I was very excited to be in a place where I knew God had called me and I felt accepted. All the hurt, bitterness, anger, and hatred that had built up inside me started dissolving.

As I served and loved on families who felt like there was no hope, families who felt like it was all over for them, God began to heal me. I want the families I work with to believe in themselves.

My dream is to one day open a ranch and have as many children and horses as possible. I want it to be a safe place where kids who are in the foster-care system can learn about themselves, appreciate the life God has given them, and know that they can be a positive influence in the world.

Finding Peace through Service

When you are willing to walk on water, God will surprise you with unforeseen blessings in your inner life. Lindsay, who works for Project Prevention, knows what that's like. God has used her acts of service to provide peace and healing in an area she had struggled with for a long time. She says,

I came to the Dream Center after I found myself in the midst of an abusive living situation and had nowhere to turn. I was a nanny working for a single father who was trying to make a better life for his son. The boy's mother visited him regularly. Through my involvement, his parents were able to provide him a safe and healthy environment for about three years. Then things began to unravel. The father fell back into his old lifestyle of drugs and crime. He became very violent, especially toward me. I finally left to get help for myself through the Dream Center's discipleship program.

Though I found a lot of healing and was truly blessed there, I couldn't stop thinking about the little boy I had cared for. I struggled with the fact that I had failed to keep his family together. Shortly after I arrived at the Dream Center, I learned that his dad had been put in jail and the boy eventually ended up in foster care.

I started working with Project Prevention. One day as I was loading the truck to head out and visit our families, I was once again struck with grief and pain over the little boy I had tried but failed to help. Suddenly God spoke to me in a way that I will never forget. He showed me that I was now doing for twenty families per week what I couldn't do for one family in three years. He was using my willingness and passion for children to accomplish far more than I had been doing on my own! That day I found the peace I longed for. I never imagined that I would find it in the midst of giving and serving others, but that is exactly where the blessing and healing came from for me!

God's Thoughts on Serving

I think Isaiah 58 encompasses the idea of how helping people in need pleases God and also offers the incredible personal benefits we can reap as a result.

Verses 2 through 5 remind me of the Christian who attends church and goes through the motions, but doesn't have a heart to help God's hurting people. God is very clear that He is not moved by this kind of behavior. "They . . . seem delighted to learn all about me. They act like a righteous nation . . . pretending they want to be near me. 'We have fasted before you!' they say. 'Why aren't you impressed?' . . . It's because you are fasting to please yourselves. Even while you fast, you keep oppressing your workers. . . . Do you really think this will please the LORD?"

Verses 6 and 7 describe what does impress God, in particular helping those in need. "This is the kind of fasting I want: Free those who are wrongly imprisoned; lighten the burden of those who work for you. Let the oppressed go free, and remove the chains that bind people. Share your food with the hungry, and give shelter to the homeless. Give clothes to those who need them, and do not hide from relatives who need your help."

Finally, in verses 8 through 12 we have a beautiful list of personal benefits that come when we help relieve social injustice—salvation, healing, direction to move forward, protection, God's ear to answer prayer requests *quickly*, relief from oppression, being light in darkness, renewed strength, limitless endurance, and a good name. Wow! God guarantees us these things if we willingly step forward in faith and serve others. Believing these promises would certainly make a difference in our personal struggles, suffering, and obstacles.

I think about the Israelites and their long journey to the Promised Land. After God delivered them from Egypt, they wandered in the wilderness for forty years. They should have arrived at their destination in eleven days. I believe that instead of living as children of God and going about doing, acting, and giving the way God commanded them, they chose to live with a slave mentality. They exhibited certain qualities that prevented them from reaching their promised destination.

Here are nine lessons you can learn while serving others that will strengthen your character and increase your faith. These truths will keep you from a life of wasted years, regret, and repeated cycles of struggle and brokenness.

As you start working with people in need, you will find that many of them have negative attitudes. It's easy to see why they have been stuck in their situations for so long. But before we can help someone else, let's make sure we take all of the planks out of our own eyes. It's much easier to model a life lived in wholeness than to try to teach principles you haven't experienced on your own.

When you serve others, you will learn to:

- Stand firm and steady
- Stop complaining
- Remember God's goodness
- Get a better perspective

- Stop feeling entitled
- Leave the past behind
- Believe that He'll take care of you
- Always be teachable
- Respect your leaders

Stand Firm and Steady

When you serve others—give to the poor, help a widow, save a child from entering the foster-care system, contribute to a cause to provide clean water, volunteer for an organization— you are constantly aware of God's hand at work. You don't just hear about miracles—you personally witness them. You see how faithful God is and that evidence inspires you to keep believing and hold on to His promises. It was something the Israelites refused to do.

Moses was called to lead the people out of Egypt, out of slavery and bondage. God gave him a promise. "I will raise my hand and strike the Egyptians. . . . And I will cause the Egyptians to look favorably on you. They will give you gifts when you go so you will not leave empty-handed" (Exodus 3:20-21).

This promise wasn't immediately fulfilled. Pharaoh, the Egyptian leader, refused to let the people of Israel go. As their confidence waned, God's people started disbelieving the promise of God and turned against Moses, accusing him of putting a sword into the Egyptians' hands in order to kill them (Exodus 5:21). The brutality of their slavery discouraged them (Exodus 6:9).

Despite their fears and doubts, God came through on His word. Moses led them out of Egypt and they left, as God promised, with some pretty amazing parting gifts from their captors (Exodus 12:35-36).

Whenever I serve on a food truck site or with Adopt-A-Block, I come across many people who have needs. I constantly tell them about God's promises that are relevant to their particular situations. When they accept the message and start trusting God, I see prayers answered. Not only do they receive God's promises, but those same promises are ingrained deeper into my own heart.

I remember when the city of Los Angeles attempted to take our building and turn it into a high school. Legally, they could seize the land for the public good according to the right of eminent domain. I stood fast in prayer with others at the Dream Center and even people in the community. I stood firm in my faith. I held on to God's promises, believing that He had given us this campus to help the people of Los Angeles. The public council meeting to resolve this issue was full of supporters on our behalf. And in the end, we were able to keep the building and continue serving others.

I believe that in the process of encouraging others to keep the faith, my own is strengthened. It's what has helped me to stand unwaveringly during challenging seasons.

Stop Complaining

Before the people of Israel had gone very far, Pharaoh changed his mind. He gathered his army and began to chase down God's people, initiating their forty years of complaints.

As Pharaoh approached, panic ensued. They cried out to the Lord, then targeted Moses, "Why did you bring us out here to die in the wilderness? Weren't there enough graves for us in Egypt? What have you done to us? . . . It's better to be a slave in Egypt than a corpse in the wilderness!" (Exodus 14:10-12).

Why were they so worried? Why do we complain instead of trust?

When God parted the Red Sea for His people's safe passage and drowned their pursuers, the people of Israel once again "put their faith in the LORD" (Exodus 14:31).

Unfortunately, their awe was short-lived. They never stopped complaining and continued to flip-flop between praising God and grumbling. I believe that had the Israelites been helping others, their complaints would have all but disappeared.

There is something about serving that shines a spotlight on just how petty our complaints are. We realize that other people have it so much worse than we do. A friend of mine who works in an orphanage in Haiti says that many people who live in the city actually consider the orphans privileged because they receive food, clothing, and an education. In fact, parents even beg the orphanage to take their children in, not because they don't love them, but so they can be provided for.

I learned a lesson while serving on the food truck one morning. Someone had donated pallets of individual-sized bags of cheese popcorn to distribute. I was thrilled, thinking, *What a great after-school treat for the kids waiting in line with their parents!*

It wasn't until the last parent was handed groceries that I noticed it. There was popcorn everywhere! Orange kernels littered the concrete, filling every crack. It was as if the heavens had opened up and rained popcorn. I was steaming! And when I realized there was only one broom in the truck, I became even more irritated. It would take me forever to clean up the mess.

I clutched the wooden broom handle and began sweeping it every which way, clearing the street and sidewalk. Suddenly, a sense of gratitude filled my heart. I thanked God for providing us with another week of food. As the popcorn kernels landed in my hair and stuck to my jeans, I thanked God for letting me be a part of this awe-inspiring ministry. By the time I reached the end of the block and turned the corner, God met me in a powerful and incredible way. His presence filled every inch of my heart, just as the popcorn had filled every part of the street.

I've been blessed to have many similar experiences in church and in some of the most inspiring conferences I've attended around the world. But they all pale in comparison to how God touched my heart doing something as simple as cleaning up popcorn. God turned my complaints into praise.

You can't help but be thankful for what you have when you are serving people less fortunate than you. A thankful heart is a happy heart that is so full there's no room for complaints. Adopt an attitude of gratitude.

Remember God's Goodness

The Israelites suffered from short-term memory. One minute they were excited and praised God for His provision and miracles. But as soon as the next challenge came, they reverted to panic mode. They whined and complained. They forgot what God was capable of and how His faithfulness never wavered.

Many times in the Old Testament God's people are encouraged to write down and tell their children all of the miracles God performed for their families. I think this is important for us to do today. Literally count your blessings. Write down every miracle and every answered prayer. Read this list over and over. Continually keep it before you. When you remember God's goodness, you will never complain.

Cindy was serving at the Dream Center when her mother was diagnosed with a brain tumor. Even through this difficult time, serving gave her hope and reminded her that God is still good. She recalls,

I grew up with a single mom who loved me dearly. My mom heard about the Dream Center and started bringing me to the youth services and the hip-hop dance classes being offered there. I started volunteering as much as I could and eventually became a full-time volunteer.

After my second year as a volunteer, my mom was diagnosed with a brain tumor. My faith was shaken. For the first time I started doubting that God loved me and would come through. During the three months that we waited for her to have surgery, I volunteered for various outreaches nearly every day. God was answering prayers and performing miracles for the people we were reaching out to. It reminded me that God was good and that there was hope for my mom. If He could perform miracles for them, then surely He could do the same for me.

My mother made it through the surgery. During her eight-month recovery, I continued to serve. Helping others brought me through this very tough and scary season. It renewed my faith and hope in God's goodness.

It's hard for me not to remember God's goodness. He has been so faithful over the years. I am so thankful for what God has done for me in my life, especially as I serve others. He has blessed me with the personal benefits listed in Isaiah 58—salvation, healing, protection, and renewed strength. I love thanking God for all He has done. And I know how much He loves to hear our praise and thanksgiving.

Get a Better Perspective

Let's face it: life is hard for every one of us to varying degrees. At some point, you'll probably be dealt some devastating blows.

But as you serve others, you will find people who have been or are experiencing far worse situations. As you interact with them, you will see God's hand at work as He faithfully and deeply heals their hearts. In fact, you will see God transform them so much that they adopt a positive attitude and are not negatively affected by their trials or discouraged by what the future holds. If you're struggling in your own life, this attitude of gratitude can transform your perspective too.

Merrilee has been a case manager for homeless families at the Dream Center for years. She committed to make a difference in the lives of others even when she went through a difficult time in her personal life. God used that experience to bless her in more ways than she could ever have imagined. Merrilee says,

> I have had the privilege of going to the Dream Center for the past ten years. When my husband and I first started attending, we were overwhelmed by the opportunities to serve in the community. We both wanted to quit our corporate jobs and go into full-time ministry. We couldn't believe the needs of people all around our community and the opportunities that were available to fill and meet those needs through our new church. As time went on, we began to understand that we were needed in the corporate world to be a light and to also generate an income to help fund the ministries at the Dream Center.
>
> When I became pregnant with twins, I quit my corporate job and became a full-time mom. About three years ago our church opened up a floor in the Dream Center devoted to homeless families. My heart broke at the thought of these children sleeping in the park or in

cars because they didn't have a home to go to. I knew that this was something I wanted to be a part of. I began volunteering as a case manager for several of the families, meeting with them weekly. Through goal setting, mentoring, and accountability, we work together to get them transitioned back into their own homes and independent living.

Serving in this capacity has truly changed my life. I get the chance to see firsthand what God can do in the lives of these families. Most of these people come in broken and discouraged. I watch their lives start to change as they begin to receive love and acceptance. I see them learn and make new choices that can positively affect their future. I can never doubt the restoring power of Jesus Christ because I get to witness it with these families.

I also see my personal life so much differently. Last year I went through some real struggles in my marriage. My initial reaction was to stay home and feel sorry for myself. However, I had made a commitment to these families and needed to show up every week. It was the best therapy I could ever have received. It is amazing how small your problems can seem when you begin to really see what other people are dealing with. As I prayed and believed for these families, it strengthened my faith during my own trials. I began to focus on the positive aspects of my marriage and not the problems.

Being able to serve these families has blessed me far more than it has blessed them. They have shown me the power of resilience and the determination to not give up. Serving others has increased my compassion for the hurts and needs of people. It has opened my eyes to what is really important and lasting in life and encouraged me to put my energy into those things while balancing the joys of being a mother and wife.

Stop Feeling Entitled

Entitlement is a dangerous, crippling attitude. It says, "I was so wronged that everyone should pay. I deserve recompense." I have seen people use their hardships as an excuse their entire life. Yes, life is unfair and sometimes people can say and do terrible things to us. But too many expect God or others to coddle them or give them handouts as a result, essentially payment for their troubles.

I have seen firsthand how a sense of entitlement can lead to unhealthy behaviors. People with this attitude tend to depend on world systems instead of God as their provider and source of all things. They carry themselves in a way that pushes people and opportunities away. They remain stuck because they are waiting for things to happen instead of being proactive and initiating change.

There is an indescribable thrill in accomplishing and overcoming on your own, with God's help. It's rewarding, even more than being given a free ticket because you think you deserve it. Does a good parent give his child everything she asks for just because she wants it? No. A good parent knows when to say no and when to empower his child to get what she wants on her own.

The apostle Paul wrote,

I pray that from his glorious, unlimited resources he will empower you with inner strength through his Spirit. Then Christ will make his home in your hearts as you trust in him. Your roots will grow down into God's love and keep you strong. And may you have the power to understand, as all God's people should, how wide, how long, how high, and how deep his love is. May you experience the love of Christ, though it is too great to understand fully. Then you will be made complete with all the fullness of life and power that comes from God.

EPHESIANS 3:16-19

God gives us the tools to lead a full life. But not necessarily on a silver platter.

Leave the Past Behind

Focusing your attention on the past can be unhealthy. The Israelites were notorious for using the past as a reason to complain in the present. "There, too, the whole community of Israel complained about Moses and Aaron. 'If only the LORD had killed us back in Egypt,' they moaned. 'There we sat around pots filled with meat and ate all the bread we wanted. But now you have brought us into this wilderness to starve us all to death'" (Exodus 16:2-3). Had they been serving others, the Israelites would have been reaping all the benefits and they would never have looked back.

When you obsess over the past—whether it was good or bad, full of hurt or even great accomplishments—you can cripple your present and limit your future. At the Dream Center we have experienced major miracles and exciting opportunities every year. From the first time we opened the doors until now, we could have stopped and patted ourselves on the back for past accomplishments. But by not dwelling on yesterday's achievements and because God is constantly surprising us with more than we could ever imagine, we look forward to growing and doing more. It's exciting to think what else God has in store for us if we continue to help those He has asked us to serve.

In Luke 9:62 Jesus says, "Anyone who puts a hand to the plow and then looks back is not fit for the Kingdom of God." God clearly has no desire or need for us to look back. That move will only keep us from where He wants us to go.

Maybe you are hesitant to step out in faith and walk on water because you fear that your past will come back to haunt you. One of the promises in Isaiah 58:8 is that "the glory of the LORD will protect you from behind." Many people who graduate from our discipleship program commit a year of their life to the Dream Center and give back through service. And many of these people have told me that somehow—no doubt through a miracle—their entire criminal record has been cleared. I'm not saying this will happen to everyone, but I can stand firm on the promise that God will not allow people's past to prevent them from boldly moving forward into the future He has in store for them.

Believe That He'll Take Care of You

Jesus said, "Don't worry about these things, saying, 'What will we eat? What will we drink? What will we wear?' These things dominate the thoughts of unbelievers, but your heavenly Father already knows all your needs. Seek the Kingdom of God above all else, and live righteously, and he will give you everything you need" (Matthew 6:31-33).

God takes care of us. He promises to in His Word. I have experienced God's provision in small ways and big ways throughout my entire journey. Not only has God taken care of my basic needs, like food and clothing, He has shown up and cared for me through those I serve.

I like how 2 Corinthians 9:12-14 reads in *The Message*: "Carrying out this social relief work involves far more than helping meet the bare needs of poor Christians. . . . This relief offering is a prod to live at your very best, showing your gratitude to God by being openly obedient to the . . . Message of Christ. You show your gratitude through your generous offerings to your needy brothers and sisters, and really toward everyone. Meanwhile, moved by the extravagance of God in your lives, they'll respond by praying for you in passionate intercession for whatever you need."

I have experienced this "passionate intercession" in my own life. Years ago, I was praying for a family member in trouble. Though I tried to help her several times, I realized I was only hurting her by stepping in and trying to save her. I had to let her reach rock bottom. It was painful. I was worried she'd die before she turned her life around. But I had to trust God.

Some of the people in our recovery program heard about this woman and started praying with me for her. Two months later, she entered that very program. It's amazing how God can use the same people you help to bless, encourage, and provide for you. And to show you how much He cares.

One of our volunteers for Ramona Gardens, an Adopt-A-Block site, learned about God's provisions as she taught young women about true love relationships, God's love, and the importance of purity. The volunteer's passion to reach broken girls stemmed from her own brokenness. Here's her story:

As a child, I never knew what real love was. My mom frequently brought home "trophies"—male and female lovers. I never really knew it was wrong.

When I was five years old, one of my mom's lovers

started raping me. This went on for nine years. When I finally discovered the message of Jesus, how He died for us and showed us the true meaning of everlasting love, I began to slowly heal. I knew that I wanted to teach about love to others who had not been shown true love.

Today I am the site leader of Ramona Gardens. About a year ago, I prayed about what I could do for the young ladies who lived there. God placed a vision in my heart to teach these girls about His pure and everlasting love. Most of the girls in the projects didn't grow up with fathers. If they did, those fathers were always in and out of the home or sexually abused the girls.

With the help of other volunteers like Yoshi and Mary, we started three-month-long classes covering topics like dating, boundaries, and purity. At the end of the three months, we planned on throwing the girls a ball to celebrate their graduation and honor their commitment to purity. I wanted the girls to have the time of their lives, but it was expensive. I needed to provide purity rings, dresses, food, escorts, a venue, and a photographer. I didn't know how we could afford it all. At the same time, four other sites agreed to teach these classes and participate in the ball. My dream was getting bigger.

Miraculously, God began to provide. Jonah, one of the leaders at the Dream Center, helped secure a venue and encouraged the women at Angelus Temple to donate dresses. But I still had to come up with the funds to buy the rings, food, and flowers. I started to stress because with bills, gasoline usage, and my own life to handle, I knew I couldn't do it alone.

God opened a door through social networking, and

many generous people, including my mother and previous site leaders from Ramona Gardens, donated funds. The offering my mother gave was a sign of her healing.

Things began to fall into place the closer we got to the event. The purity ball was amazing. Through this process, God taught me about fully trusting Him and His plans. I learned that the vision He gives me He will see through to the end. He will always work things out.

Always Be Teachable

In order to live healed and whole and carry out the dreams God has put on our hearts, we have to remain teachable—no matter how old we are. Some people feel that after a certain age, they have "arrived" and have no need to learn anything more. But there's always more to learn. Always.

Why are some life lessons so hard to learn? When we refuse to listen to God, we usually find ourselves in the same bad predicament time and time again. Hebrews 3:7-11 reminds us how important it is to listen to God:

The Holy Spirit says,

"Today when you hear his voice,
  don't harden your hearts
as Israel did when they rebelled,
  when they tested me in the wilderness.
There your ancestors tested and tried my patience,
  even though they saw my miracles for forty years.
So I was angry with them, and I said,
'Their hearts always turn away from me.
  They refuse to do what I tell them.'

So in my anger I took an oath:
  'They will never enter my place of rest.'"

God got frustrated with the Israelites because they were unteachable; they refused to listen to Him. If He got irritated with them, He must get frustrated with us.

I have learned to be open to what God can teach me through serving others. For instance, being willing has taught me to have greater compassion, to understand the plight behind a person's pain instead of making general assumptions about his or her condition. Being teachable has also strengthened my faith and freed my spirit.

Respect Your Leaders

When you complain about the leaders in your life, you are actually complaining about God. The Israelites continually turned against Moses. I'm sure there were moments he wished he could be an Egyptian prince again and punish them. I'm shocked by how often the Israelites attacked Moses and Aaron, his second in command.

Moses and Aaron said to all the people of Israel, "By evening you will realize it was the LORD who brought you out of the land of Egypt. In the morning you will see the glory of the LORD, because he has heard your complaints, which are against him, not against us. What have we done that you should complain about us?" Then Moses added, "The LORD will give you meat to eat in the evening and bread to satisfy you in the morning, for he has heard all your complaints against him. What have we done? Yes, your complaints are against the LORD, not against us."

EXODUS 16:6-8

Moses probably wouldn't have scripted his life the way God did. Moses didn't ask to be put in a basket and given to an Egyptian princess. He did not ask to encounter a talking burning bush that would give him marching orders for a scary mission. He even bargained with God to let Aaron speak on his behalf because he felt unqualified. But Moses continued to lead the people of Israel because God told him to. The man deserved some respect.

The apostle Paul wrote, "Everyone must submit to governing authorities. For all authority comes from God, and those in positions of authority have been placed there by God" (Romans 13:1).

If you work in a secular environment for someone who is not a Christian, you are still required to respect and serve him or her well. Otherwise, you are misrepresenting God and not fulfilling whatever He has you there to accomplish and learn.

We have to live our lives for God, not others. God notices our efforts even if the leaders we serve do not. Then, whatever we do, whenever we work for others as unto the Lord, we will enjoy our work and in God's time we will reap a reward. "My dear brothers and sisters, be strong and immovable. Always work enthusiastically for the Lord, for you know that nothing you do for the Lord is ever useless" (1 Corinthians 15:58).

I have always done the best I could at every job I've had, from my first job as a teenager at a clothing store, to flipping burgers at In-N-Out, to volunteering at the Dream Center. Doing the minimum just to get by isn't my style. I've always tried to be conscientious about every task and carry out responsibilities with excellence.

A Life of Service, Adventure, and Joy

I admire my father-in-law, Tommy Barnett, and am inspired by his example. He always says that he wishes he could have a hundred more years to live, to serve those in need.

Tommy's late father was one of the pioneers of the bus ministry, so it was natural for Tommy to follow in his dad's footsteps. He recognized the importance of providing transportation for people who couldn't get to church on their own, most of whom lived in lower-income neighborhoods.

When Tommy built his church in Phoenix, some of the deacons started complaining. They thought that since the congregation was growing and they were now an "established" church, it wasn't necessary to continue busing in worshipers from those neighborhoods. Tommy disagreed and lost some deacons in the process. But I'm convinced that God continues to bless Tommy because of that willingness to serve.

Do you want to be freed from regrets? To stop wallowing in your mistakes? Do you want to stop being haunted by your past? Do you want to stop repeating the same cycle of sin? Do you want to be whole and full of joy, faith, and power?

Start walking on water.

CHAPTER 11

THE GOOD KIND OF FEAR

The LORD watches over those who fear him,
those who rely on his unfailing love. He rescues them from
death and keeps them alive in times of famine.

—— PSALM 33:18-19 ——

MAKING THE CHOICE to serve others and relieve social injustice may spur certain fears. What is it going to look like? What if I can't handle it? Will it endanger my family or me? What if it costs too much?

Walking on water does require faith. The Bible tells us that without faith it's impossible to please God (Hebrews 11:6). If you're not at least a little worried or scared, you won't need much faith. But while a certain amount of fear is expected, it shouldn't turn into an excuse to not fulfill what God is calling you to do.

I remember one of my first experiences at the Dream Center. I was both excited and nervous as I headed to the gym for my first Adopt-A-Block meeting. A million thoughts flitted through my mind. *Am I prepared for what lies ahead? Will the families we're serving even accept our help?* My heart beat faster the closer I got to the entrance. I was late. As I got closer, I heard Matthew's voice, giving an introductory message to the volunteers.

Suddenly there was an earsplitting sound of screeching tires. Across the narrow street from where I stood, five police cars had swooped in and surrounded a dilapidated apartment building. The glaring red and white lights from the vehicles were blinding. It was like a scene out of a Hollywood film, except this was real life.

I panicked and ran inside the building. I looked out the doors to see what was happening outside. In a matter of a few seconds, about ten police officers, some uniformed, others in black tactical gear, leaped out of their cars and crouched behind car doors. Every one of them had high-powered assault rifles positioned on their shoulders, prepared to fire. My heart beat wildly in my chest as one officer yelled through a bullhorn at someone inside the building. I headed into the meeting after a couple of minutes but found out later that the police standoff lasted a few hours. The other volunteers hadn't a clue what was going on at the time. Later I found out that there was often police activity around that apartment. It was a normal, almost daily occurrence—nothing out of the ordinary.

This was my new reality, something my home church pastor had warned my parents about, diligently trying to convince my dad that it was too dangerous for me to work at the Dream Center. But my father knew it was safer for a person to be in the will of God than anywhere else and supported my decision. Thankfully, the neighborhood around the Dream Center has changed from the extremely violent place it was when I first arrived. But from the first day I never once doubted God's faithfulness to protect me as I served Him.

The Fear of God

Fear is not a bad thing when it's directed in a positive way. The Bible frequently talks about having a fear of God. This doesn't mean we need to be scared of God. "Fearing God" in a biblical sense simply means honoring and respecting Him in all we do.

The Bible is full of wonderful promises that center on fearing God. One of my favorite passages is Psalm 112. Here are a few other promises from Scripture:

True humility and fear of the LORD
   lead to riches, honor, and long life.
PROVERBS 22:4

The LORD is a friend to those who fear him.
PSALM 25:14

He surrounds and defends all who fear him.
PSALM 34:7

Fear the LORD, you his godly people,
   for those who fear him will have all they need.
PSALM 34:9

The LORD is like a father to his children,
   tender and compassionate to those who fear him.
PSALM 103:13

My dad says that people fear everything but God; but if they feared God instead, they'd have nothing else to fear. When you honor Him, you will have everything you need, and you will experience unexplainable joy and peace.

Living in Wisdom

Living in the fear of God means you make life choices based on the understanding that God is in control of everything and that he created, designed, and gave you whatever gifts and talents you have. In other words, you live in wisdom. Proverbs 9:10 says, "Fear of the LORD is the foundation of wisdom. Knowledge of the Holy One results in good judgment."

During one of our midweek services, Matthew and I sat next to a very wealthy man I knew of through one of our members, who was visiting for the first time. During the offering he put a check in the bucket. I couldn't help but notice the amount, but Matthew didn't see it. As the offering bucket made its way down the aisle, my husband thanked the man for the gift. The visitor was quick to respond. "It's not my money."

I admire that wise attitude. It represents a genuine fear of God. The man knew that his ability to make money and the successes he enjoyed in his business came from the Lord. He can live without worry and be excited about his future because he has aligned himself with the promises that come from fearing God.

No Need to Fear Anything

Second, living in the fear of God means we don't have to live in fear of people, circumstances, the unknown, death, or anything else that may frighten us. This is something Nehemiah understood quite well.

Nehemiah's mission was to spearhead a construction project: rebuilding the walls of Jerusalem. It was neither easy nor enthusiastically embraced. Nehemiah was mocked and threatened, and his enemies spread a rumor to create dissension against him. But Nehemiah just worked harder.

Even his friends offered him no encouragement. "Let us meet together inside the Temple of God and bolt the doors shut," they told Nehemiah. "Your enemies are coming to kill you tonight" (Nehemiah 6:10).

Nehemiah responded without wavering in his faith. "Should someone in my position run from danger? Should someone in my position enter the Temple to save his life? No, I won't do it!" (6:11). Nehemiah's fear of God produced in him boldness, confidence, steadfastness, dedication, determination, perseverance, and optimism. Having the fear of God will make you invincible. If I had been Nehemiah, I might have continued working, but I would have at least put on a helmet and a bulletproof vest.

If God is for you, you have nothing to fear. What can those who try to harm you really accomplish? Jesus said, "Don't be afraid of those who want to kill your body; they cannot do any more to you after that. But I'll tell you whom to fear. Fear God, who has the power to kill you and then throw you into hell. Yes, he's the one to fear" (Luke 12:4-5).

Sometimes when I watch the news and see the atrocities, pain, and suffering in this world, I get worked up. But then I remember what the prophet Isaiah said: "The LORD has given me a strong warning not to think like everyone else does. He said, 'Don't call everything a conspiracy, like they do, and don't live in dread of what frightens them. Make the LORD of Heaven's Armies holy in your life. He is the one you should fear. He is the one who should make you tremble. He will keep you safe'" (Isaiah 8:11-14). Talk about peace of mind and heart!

Katie, one of our volunteers, experienced some scary stuff when she started volunteering. She felt called to serve at a young age, and when she was seventeen, Katie became an intern for the Dream Center's family housing program. She lived with the families, which allowed her to experience everyday life with them. At first, everything seemed fine, but then the sentiment began to change. Looking down on her because she was so young, family members spit on her, sent her hate mail, and uttered death threats. She says,

> I remember asking God if I should stay. His response to me was so simple. *Is knowing that you are pleasing Me enough?* I told Him yes. I started to recognize the opportunity He had given me, trusting me with His children. By responding to their behaviors with kindness, I was able to show the families unconditional love. Though many of them did change for the better, some did not. I've come to understand the psychology of why people remain stuck in their attitudes. That knowledge has helped me continue to offer grace and compassion. I still help with the families at the Dream Center today and consider it such a privilege.

Living in Obedience

Finally, living in the fear of God means you obey His Word. I feel strongly about this truth. You cannot tell God that you sincerely love Him if you don't obey Him.

Here are a few verses from Leviticus that show how fearing God goes hand in hand with being obedient and helping to serve others:

> Do not insult the deaf or cause the blind to stumble. You must fear your God. (19:14)

Stand up in the presence of the elderly, and show respect for the aged. Fear your God. (19:32)

Show your fear of God by not taking advantage of each other. (25:17)

When Job experienced seemingly endless waves of tragedies, hardships, and physical ailments, he maintained his innocence. He passionately defended his case before God and told Him there was no way his suffering could have been caused by sin. Job lists the sins he did not commit, many of which had to do with helping others. He rhetorically asked,

> Have I refused to help the poor,
>   or crushed the hopes of widows?
> Have I been stingy with my food
>   and refused to share it with orphans?
> No, from childhood I have cared for orphans
>   like a father,
>   and all my life I have cared for widows.
> Whenever I saw the homeless without clothes
>   and the needy with nothing to wear,
> did they not praise me
>   for providing wool clothing to keep them warm? . . .
>
> My servants have never said,
>   "He let others go hungry."
> I have never turned away a stranger
>   but have opened my doors to everyone.
> JOB 31:16-20, 31-32

Before Angelus Temple merged with the Dream Center congregation, Matthew and I spent a Sunday with members of the new church. He preached his knockout message about finding your cause and living for others as a way to introduce us, and received an overwhelming response of people willing to make a difference.

But two women approached us after the service. Their expressions were less than enthusiastic. "We know about all the things you do to help people, but what are you going to do for us?" one of them asked. Matthew and I were stunned. In their selfishness, they completely missed the point. They believed they deserved to receive, not be asked to give.

Recently we lost a few members who believed we were focusing too much of our attention on reaching the lost and helping to heal those who struggle with addictions or other issues. If people choose to believe Matthew and I are in the wrong for being obedient to the call of God, then I'm happy to be wrong in their eyes.

If Matthew and I didn't live in the fear of God, the Dream Center would torture us with stress. But because we know we are being obedient and the organization is in God's hands, we can sleep well at night and look forward to the future.

God Shows Up When We Obey

When you live obediently, you'll find that God will protect the work He calls you to do. About ten years ago, a woman from Florida called the Dream Center and asked if we could help her and her thirteen-year-old daughter who had Down syndrome. At the time, we had not started our family program and we were neither equipped nor had the space to house them.

Although we made it clear that we had no accommodations,

she and her daughter showed up at our door a week later. Talk about being put into a jam. It was nine o'clock in the evening, so our volunteer made them comfortable in her office while she tried to figure out a solution. She started contacting nearby shelters, but every one was filled to capacity.

At one point, the thirteen-year-old daughter got up and walked into the adjacent bathroom. Because the original hospital was built on a hill, the entrance to the Dream Center is actually on the sixth floor of the building. All of a sudden, the volunteer and the girl's mother heard a loud thump. They ran into the bathroom and found the girl hanging out of the window, holding on to the windowsill six stories above the ground. The two women tried frantically to help the teenager, but it was no use. She lost her grip and fell.

The volunteer and the girl's mother ran out of the building to where the girl lay on the ground, convinced they'd find her dead. But a bush had broken her fall. She had only a single scratch on her arm.

God does not want fear to dictate our steps of willingness. He wants us to be obedient. When you step out in faith and help others, there may be times you will put yourself at risk in a scary place. But God will never fail you. We didn't know the girl had a history of jumping out of windows and running away. We were just trying to help. We were obedient and trusted God. He provided a miracle.

Oftentimes when people visit the Dream Center, they have a million what-if questions. What if people steal from you? What if someone influences others negatively? You cannot allow your fears, what-if questions, or worst-case scenarios to keep you from being obedient. Not when God's got your back.

A Memorable Anniversary

When my tenth wedding anniversary was approaching in 2009, I wanted to do something really special and unexpected for Matthew. He is almost impossible to shop for, so I needed to think outside the box.

Matthew loves all kinds of music. Sometimes during a service, before he gets up to preach, he'll do a spur-of-the-moment singing contest with members of the congregation. After one of those spontaneous sing-offs, I knew what my anniversary present would be. Either God gave me the idea or I took a crazy pill that morning. I decided to perform a medley of special songs—combining singing, playing instruments, and dancing—for my husband in front of the church, before the sermon. At that point in my life, I was still deathly afraid of being onstage and speaking in public. But I believed God was challenging me to overcome my fear with faith.

I put together my playlist. I would begin with "Kiss Me" by Sixpence None the Richer, singing and accompanying myself on the accordion, then switch to the piano to play and sing "Come What May" by Air Supply and "Two Occasions" by Babyface, and end the performance with a hip-hop dance to Fergie's "Clumsy." Are you still stuck on the fact that I said I was going to play the accordion? Yes, I do play, but let's just keep it our little secret. I used to think it was my parents' way of torturing me, but the reality is they had no idea how uncool it was for a kid to play one.

I was crazy nervous. Whenever I had played the piano or accordion in front of people before, my mind always went blank and I would make a million mistakes. I'm also not the best singer. And though I was a cheerleader in high school and had some rhythm, I was thirty years old, and dancing had changed a lot since then.

I prepared for three months. I thought this gift would either be the greatest thing or the worst thing I had ever done for Matthew. It really had the potential to go either way. The night of the performance, I paced back and forth backstage. Though a number of fears flooded my mind, I didn't dwell on them. Instead, I thanked God. I believed the performance would be a hit because I had done my part and was confident God would do the rest.

It turned out to be a huge success. I wasn't perfect by any stretch of the imagination, but I got the outcome I wanted. Matthew was completely shocked and totally flattered. My friend actually posted this video online. (I know you're dying to see it, so you can check it out at http://vimeo.com/7223906. The video is called "Caroline's Anniversary Surprise.")

There was an added surprise for me. After God pulled me through this challenge, I got over my fear of public speaking. I learned a lot through this experience about how to face my fears. The lessons I learned might be helpful to you, too.

I asked God to be involved. I know my experience wasn't the typical ministry venture, but God was involved. I find it's hard to quit when you step into something you know God is a part of.

I had a good time. I didn't want to just get through the performance. I also prayed that I would actually enjoy myself. And I did. When you serve others and make a difference, you will have a good time and even, at times, a whole lot of fun.

I saw the big picture. I constantly reminded myself of the outcome—Matthew's surprise and joy. When you help others, instead of focusing on their pain or suffering, focus on their healing. If you are helping an organization to stop human trafficking, don't be attuned solely to the emotional brokenness of the young women you help. Think of all of the goodness God will sow into their lives. Look at them as whole women living full and abundant lives and pursuing their dreams.

I told my close friends. I told a few of my friends what I was planning. They knew my fears and my inabilities. Though they thought I was nuts, none of them discouraged me. When you find a need to fill, surround yourself with people who will encourage you and champion your cause. They are the ones who will believe in and pray for you.

A caution about "dream killers." Dream killers will discourage you because they fear that your success may minimize theirs. In an effort to keep you down, they will tell you all the reasons why something can't be done. They will point out only the risks, not the rewards. They will belittle the potential for greatness and positive influence. They will paint worst-case scenarios. Though I have never severed ties with dream killers, I certainly distance myself from them.

I embraced responsibility. I confess that I hoped our worship leader would help me pull off Matthew's gift, but he wasn't able to. God wanted me to own my part and forge ahead. Though you may need other people to help you in your cause, don't shirk your responsibility to make it happen. Eliminate excuses.

I prayed away my fear. Any time I felt fear inching its way into my heart, I would pray. I like the quote, "Where your thoughts go, your power flows." When you feel afraid, instead of dwelling on that fear, turn your thoughts toward God.

I spent time with God, asking for His strength and confidence. Through experience, I have found that the amount of strength, confidence, and focus I have is directly related to how much time I spend with God.

For three months leading up to the performance, I had to

practice every single day. And every day, until I spent time with God, I would be tempted to quit. There is something about being in His presence that reminds you of what you are capable of accomplishing through Him. God reveals how He sees you, and your perspective on things shifts to a proper place. You can enjoy a peace that surpasses understanding and can walk away with a confidence that you are not doing this alone.

I prepared well. The more I practiced, the less fear I had. Worrying about whether or not you can manage what God is calling you to do is a detriment. Preparing, learning, and doing your homework is a benefit.

I reminded myself that God is on my side. In my head, I sounded like a motivational speaker every day during that season. I quoted Philippians 4:13 and 2 Timothy 1:7 for encouragement.

Breaking Fear's Hold

There are so many suffering and hurting people who are desperate for the love that you have to give. There are those who have answered the call God gave them and are also trying to carry the load of others who are held back by fear. The need cannot be handled by just a faithful few.

Patricia and Brian share a beautiful, loving commitment to each other and to God. While they were engaged, Patricia was in a car accident and was paralyzed from the neck down. She wanted to break the engagement, not wanting to be a burden to Brian or prevent him from having a family of his own one day. But Brian's love won her over and they married. Soon after, they started volunteering at a food truck site. Patricia would sit in the truck reading her Bible and praying for us, while Brian distributed food.

About six years ago, in the face of fear and uncertainty, they felt led to adopt. They took in an eighteen-month-old boy who was found in an abandoned car. The baby had drugs in his system, but with Pat and Brian's loving care, he became healthy. A few years later, Pat and Brian were contacted by social services. The social worker told them that a biological brother of their adopted son had been found. With joy, they adopted that little boy too. Today this family of four is happy, healthy, and whole. Had Patricia and Brian not stepped out beyond their fears, they would not have been the miracle these brothers needed.

Alena is one of my heroes. She has fostered over 130 kids in the last twenty years. She started fostering as a single mother of three small girls. Her husband had left her because their youngest daughter was in the hospital the first year of her life, and he felt his wife spent too much time there. One day while visiting her daughter, Alena noticed that the baby in the bed next to her daughter's never had visitors. She found out the baby was terminally ill and was a ward of the state. That moment she made the choice to become a foster parent.

Talk about being fearless—Alena told me a story about a boy she had taken in who was seven years old. When he was four, he saw his father kill his mother. When the boy called 911, his father beat him. By the time he came to live with Alena, the boy had been in over twenty-five foster homes in a span of three years, moved around because of his fits of rage.

Still, Alena believed she was called to foster this boy. Sadly, when the boy almost killed one of her daughters, Alena had to contact the authorities and let the police take him to a psychiatric facility. Alena has not given up on this child. She still believes there is hope for him to have a good, healthy, and purposeful life.

Alena was willing and found great joy in answering her call to be a foster parent. But even with a willing heart, we are sometimes limited by circumstances. Be wise about what you can and cannot do.

Putting Fear in Its Place

I'll admit there were times in my life when fear got the best of me, and I backed away from personal challenges and things I felt God calling me to do. Matthew often has opportunities to be on television and meet influential and well-known people. He's asked me on many occasions to join him. I used to say no because I was worried I'd stumble on my words or stick my foot in my mouth. But now I say yes when I can. There have also been times when I've seen a hurting person in a public place and felt God ask me to do something—like pray for her or pay for the items of the person frantically counting pennies in front of me at the grocery checkout.

Most of the time, I was reluctant to jump in. It's not that I didn't want to help—doing so would put me out on a limb. How would the person react? Maybe she'd think I was crazy. I allowed fear to overwhelm me, and I backed away from those God-appointed opportunities. Today, fear does not control me or my actions. If I feel God telling me to do something outside of my comfort zone, I willingly step out.

Second Timothy 1:7 says, "God has not given us a spirit of fear and timidity, but of power, love, and self-discipline." Do not let fear hold you back from serving others in the area of your trigger. Do not allow missed opportunities to lead to a life of regret. Do not allow fear to dictate your steps. Allow God, and Him alone, to determine your future. When you live in the fear of God, you will live a free and powerful life.

CHAPTER 12

THE POWER OF ONE

God is not unjust; he will not forget your work and the love you have shown him as you have helped his people and continue to help them.

——————— HEBREWS 6:10, NIV ———————

I BELIEVE THAT ONE individual can make a difference. Romans 5:18-19 tells us, "Yes, Adam's one sin brings condemnation for everyone, but Christ's one act of righteousness brings a right relationship with God and new life for everyone. Because one person disobeyed God, many became sinners. *But because one other person obeyed God, many will be made righteous*" (emphasis added).

All you need to make a difference is to obey God and be willing to step out and serve those in need. That's it! If you are willing, you can prevent a child from dying of starvation. You can prevent men and women from going hungry. You can prevent a family from being torn apart. You can prevent a teenager from struggling in school because of not being able to read. You can prevent someone from being homeless. The God of heaven, who is the same yesterday, today, and forever; who parted the sea for Moses; stopped the sun for Joshua; and raised Jesus from the dead, is the same God who loves you, is on your side, and fights for you.

What One Can Do

History has been shaped by influential people, both negatively and positively. Time and time again, one person has done something that has affected many others. Remember the *Invisible Children* documentary I mentioned in chapter 1? A woman, Alice "Lakwena" Auma, began the insurgency called the Holy Spirit movement, against the government in Uganda in 1986, leading a rebellion that Joseph Kony inherited. Because of her initial efforts, untold millions have been murdered, displaced, and abducted in the last twenty-six years, and the numbers continue to grow because the war is still going on.

Margaret Sanger founded Planned Parenthood, an organization that performs 1.2 million abortions in the United States every year.[26] Not only are babies killed, but the women who terminate their pregnancies suffer emotional brokenness.

Thankfully, there are many people who have championed outstanding positive causes. I am fortunate to have had the chance to meet current world changers such as . . .

> ‣ Blake Mycoskie, founder of TOMS shoes. As of September, 2010, TOMS has given over a million pairs of shoes to children in need around the world.[27]
> ‣ Scott Harrison, founder of Charity: Water. This organization has funded 6,185 projects that will provide clean water for an estimated 2,545,000 people.[28]
> ‣ Marilyn and Gary Skinner, who started the Watoto Childcare Ministries in Uganda, restoring hope and dignity and providing education, healthcare, and spiritual development for children orphaned by AIDS.[29]
> ‣ Joyce Meyer, whose ministry includes Hand of Hope, which feeds seventy thousand hungry people around

the world every day. In addition, she has contributed
$10.9 million to disaster relief funds.[30]

▸ Hal Donaldson with Convoy of Hope, who has
distributed $304 million worth of food and supplies and
served more than 55 million people in need through
international children's feeding initiatives, community
outreaches, disaster response, and partner resourcing.[31]

▸ Nancy Alcorn, founder of Mercy Ministries, who
established four women's recovery homes, with affiliates
in the United Kingdom, Canada, and New Zealand. In
a survey conducted in 2008, 93 percent of respondents
said that Mercy Ministries helped transform their lives
and restore their hope.[32]

▸ Christine Caine, founder of the A21 Campaign, who
has created and instituted a fourfold approach to abolish
sex trafficking. Their ministry has partnered with law
enforcement for the prosecution and conviction of sex
traffickers in the Ukraine and Greece.[33]

▸ And my personal favorite, Matthew Barnett, founder of
the Dream Center (wink!).[34]

And the list could go on and on, organizations throughout
the world that are making a difference in millions of people's
lives because one person was willing to step out and speak up.

All of these amazing leaders have found their trigger. They
took the time to look long enough to be compelled into action.
Though the injustice they are helping to eliminate breaks their
hearts, they have also found great joy and satisfaction in being a
part of the solution. Know what I've noticed about them? They
are confident and at peace. They live a big life with an eye on
what's really important.

We *Can* Make a Difference

No matter how daunting the amount of suffering is in this world or the number of people who are in need, we in the Christian army are not outnumbered. I believe the biggest injustice is that although these problems would be easy for us to fix, we haven't yet done so. I think about the statistic I mentioned earlier— 18.5 million orphaned children around the world. With over two billion believers in the global community, it would take less than one percent of willing Christians to adopt these kids and every orphan would have a home.

You might be scared that God is asking you to be part of that one percent. Remember, God wants what you want. If He puts an issue on your heart that requires your willingness, that passion will ultimately override your fear. Take it from me and so many others: when God asks you to do something, you'll quickly discover that you can't say no. It's all you'll think about!

Get Others Involved

If you're inspired, recruit your friends or members of your community to champion your cause. Get them involved and marvel in the collective effort you can make.

Take a cue from the efforts of the early church. "All the believers were united in heart and mind. And they felt that what they owned was not their own, so they shared everything they had. The apostles testified powerfully to the resurrection of the Lord Jesus, and God's great blessing was upon them all. There were no needy people among them, because those who owned land or houses would sell them and bring the money to the apostles to give to those in need" (Acts 4:32-35). What an example for us to follow today. The early Christians worked together as a unified front. And as a result, no one around them was in need.

It might sound a little extreme to sell your property or your home. But I don't believe these followers of Christ sold all they owned and were homeless or lacked necessities. The Bible doesn't tell us that they gave so much that their lifestyle had to change. They were simply willing to give freely and with a cheerful heart.

Be Willing

All of my close friends help serve others and make a difference in some way. They use their time, energy, and passions to love on others. I am proud and blessed to have friends who put their willingness into action as volunteers.

With seven-year-old twins, a husband, a home, and a number of pets (I can't keep track of how many because she is always taking more in—a great sign of a willing spirit!), my friend Merrilee is always busy. For the last few years, she's been helping out at the Dream Center as a case manager for a few families living on our family floor. Her caring involvement will change the direction not only of their immediate future, but for generations to come. Merrilee treats these families as her own and is proud when they make strides—big and small—to better their lives.

Leah, a wife and a mother of two young boys, owns a small business with her husband. Every few months, her whole family volunteers for an intense week or two at the Dream Center, tackling large projects. Recently, the family joined the volunteer crew to paint the exterior of the church, saving us $60,000.

Danise looks way too young to have two grown kids. Most of the time, she helps her husband with his landscaping business. But once a week, Danise drives an hour to help at the Dream Center. She serves as a women's counselor and teaches an evening Bible study. (Check out her blog at http://danisejurado.com.)

Start Simply

Don't allow insecurities or feelings of inadequacy or not having a full-time position in ministry to prevent you from stepping out and walking on water. Don't underestimate what you can bring to the table when God is involved.

Do something as simple as taking time to teach someone to read. It will change not only their future but their children's future. Taking the time to teach a struggling young woman about finances and budgeting might be what changes her life from merely surviving to thriving. Teaching a foster child or young adult in an impoverished community to cook could ignite a passion that may turn into a successful career. Using your extra time to clean a single mother's house may be the momentary respite she needs to keep her from having a nervous breakdown. Your hug might be what breaks preconceived beliefs of racism.

A friend of mine started her own Adopt-A-Block program in Sweden. While the area in which she serves doesn't have the same needs as those in Los Angeles, she has found that loneliness is a major need. Simply visiting with people has given them hope that they matter to someone and to God and has breathed life back into their souls.

I don't know what God has laid on your heart. I don't know what your trigger is. I don't know where your passion lies. The most important thing is to begin somewhere. Do some research online. Contact and talk to people who are on the front lines, making a difference. Start close to home and look around your own neighborhood. Find a need that you can fill or a way to help someone. Support a cause financially or in other ways. If necessary, be willing to get your hands dirty.

Fight On

Though I believe beyond a shadow of a doubt that we can make a difference, individually and collectively, I'm not naive. I know there are times when serving others doesn't yield the positive results everyone expects. Sometimes the people you help refuse to help themselves. There may be days when it seems like your efforts are futile and your time has been wasted. It's easy to get discouraged and give up, but I want to encourage you to keep on walking.

What if the single mother you sacrifice so much time, attention, and maybe even finances for doesn't change her life and ends up pregnant again? You have every right to feel used and taken advantage of. But do you quit? Of course not! You might have to make adjustments to the way you help, but you keep on serving.

Everyone has a different way of accepting opportunities to improve themselves or their situation. Some people graciously accept help and are willing to do whatever it takes to get better. Other folks don't value the opportunity, squander it, and feel entitled to get another one.

We have taken in some extremely broken people at the Dream Center. They are broken by circumstances out of their control or by bad choices they have made. Sometimes both. There have been moments when I've tried so hard to help someone but to no avail. I've been tempted to give up and let some other program, team, or person do it. But I know that God is the One who can change them, and I must remain hopeful that He will.

When those you serve don't appreciate your help, continue to serve with a thankful heart. Let it be a reminder of how gracious and merciful God has been to you. Regardless of the outcome of your commitment to serve others, you will still reap the benefits God has promised to those who serve.

The Joys of Serving

There is an indescribable joy that comes from being obedient. When all is said and done, you have willingly been part of a greater cause.

I remember the day Matthew came home from a grueling fund-raising trip and immediately headed to Ramona Gardens, an Adopt-A-Block site.

The little girls at the site's weekly Bible study painted his fingernails to make him an "official part" of their team. He feasted on delicious spicy beans and rice with the families. He was encouraged by what the handful of teenage girls who were going through our church's purity classes were doing to change their lives. When Matthew came home that night, he was beaming.

On that day I discovered that Matthew's best days in ministry had nothing to do with preaching in large arenas or megachurches in front of hundreds of thousands of people. It had nothing to do with hobnobbing with celebrities or being a guest on a major television network news channel. His favorite days were being with and loving those who had nothing to give him other than themselves.

Reaping Eternal Rewards

I feel compelled to serve others because I know I am investing my time, efforts, and energy into something that is eternal and cannot be destroyed. Something that cannot rust, get old, break down, or go out of style. Jesus encourages us, "Don't store up treasures here on earth, where moths eat them and rust destroys them, and where thieves break in and steal. Store your treasures in heaven, where moths and rust cannot destroy, and thieves do not break in and steal. Wherever your treasure is, there the desires of your heart will also be" (Matthew 6:19-21).

One day when I was working at a site with group of short-term missions team volunteers, a woman said, "Caroline, I've seen you here for a couple of years doing the same thing. You're a bright and beautiful young lady. When are you finally going to do something real with your life? When are you going to go to college or work on your career? Or have enough money to buy a house or make investments?"

I'm sure she had good intentions with her questions, but I was taken aback. What each of us does at the Dream Center isn't for the here and now; it's for eternity. Our food truck ministry, for instance, is not just about handing out food. We use food as a tool to draw people closer to God and to offer them the gift of salvation.

I told her that though I appreciated her concerns, I felt called to full-time ministry. As the woman walked away, I felt sorry for her and her limited vision of what this life is about. Who cares if I never go to college? Who cares if I never own a home? Who cares if I couldn't buy fancy new clothes? Who cares if my car was made the same year I was born? I know God doesn't. Material things and humanly devised plans are mere shadows of the treasures that are stored up in heaven, treasures of soul significance stored in the broken clay pots of our lives.

God has a funny way of bringing things full circle. Today I have a house, new clothes, a car that's younger than I am—all those material things—but I didn't have to get them working twelve hours a day outside of my calling at the Dream Center. And as nice as my new car is, I accomplished a lot of ministry with my Volvo clunker.

God doesn't call each and every one of us into full-time mission work or ministry. And certainly there is nothing wrong with having a house, a car, nice clothes, or a career or job outside of the church. We just need to live to impact people for eternity. This goal is the same for a stay-at-home mom, a CEO, a youth pastor, or a student. Investing in the lives of others and being a variable in any equation that fills a need is what truly matters.

Everything You Do Matters

Use whatever willingness you have. And know that it will change, depending on the season in your life. Don't become stressed if you can't give or do more at certain times in your life. The key to being a good and faithful servant of God is to continually give and do what God calls you to give and do.

If you are willing to donate a hundred dollars a year to a charity or volunteer once a week, do it. Everything counts. Every act of obedience makes a difference because God will always multiply your efforts. Jesus fed a crowd of five thousand with five loaves and two fish that a little boy was willing to give. If he hadn't been willing to give what little he had, all five thousand people would have gone hungry that day.

Don't worry if you don't have the resources, either. You don't have to have a big building, a warehouse of food, or a multi-million-dollar budget to walk on water. God can use you in miraculous ways to make life better one person at a time.

I like the apostle Paul's words:

I thought I should send these brothers ahead of me to make sure the gift you promised is ready. But I want it to be a willing gift, not one given grudgingly.

Remember this—a farmer who plants only a few seeds will get a small crop. But the one who plants generously will get a generous crop. *You must each decide in your heart how much to give. And don't give reluctantly or in response to pressure.* "For God loves a person who gives cheerfully." And God will generously provide all you need. *Then* you will always have everything you need and plenty left over to share with others. As the Scriptures say,

"They share freely and give generously to the poor.
  Their good deeds will be remembered forever."
2 CORINTHIANS 9:5-9 (EMPHASIS ADDED)

There are so many remarkable opportunities for you to be a part of the healing that needs to take place in this world. The great news is that all you need is the willingness to do it. Become God's ambassador during your lifetime. Find your post and fill your position.

Walking on water is not just a story in the Bible. It's a reality. It's a way to live life with purpose.

It's time to get out of the boat.

Acknowledgments

To . . .

My Lord and Savior Jesus Christ for loving me more than I can ever understand and for giving me the grace to live this life.

Matthew—it's because of your willingness to step out in obedience and walk on water that the Dream Center exists today. Your commitment to God and His calling has given countless leaders, volunteers, and me the means to walk out our own calling and causes. I love you with all my heart.

Mia and Caden—thank you for giving Mommy the time, love, and patience to write this book. I love you both so very much.

My parents, Clarence and Anja, who raised me in a God-fearing and God-loving home.

My sisters, Bernice, Cathy, and Robin, who taught me love, joy, peace, patience, kindness, goodness, faithfulness, gentleness, and self-control . . . love.

My father-in-law, Tommy Barnett, who opened my eyes to see a bigger God.

Todd Leader, who has made our family and ministry life so much better and more productive than we could have ever been on our own.

Korrin Coahran, for helping me to be two people.

All the wonderful men and women who were willing to be vulnerable and open, for sharing your stories in this book. Know that your testimony and great work being done for the Lord changes lives every day.

Everyone on the Tyndale team who worked so hard to help make this book what it is. I appreciate your talents, creativity, and belief in me.

A. J. Gregory, for bringing to the table the experience and ability that I did not have.

Esther Fedorkevich, for representing me and my vision.

Discussion Guide

Chapter 1: Willing

1. "I passionately wanted to work for God," Caroline says, "but I wasn't bold enough to preach the gospel on a street corner. I desperately wanted to make a difference for Christ and was frustrated because I didn't know *what* to do." Can you relate to this? In what way?

2. How does God's answer to Caroline's question about the injustice in the world surprise her?

3. What do you think of when you hear the term "social justice"? What examples of injustice do you see in the world and/or in your own community? Can you relate to Caroline's feeling of being overwhelmed in the face of it and not knowing where to begin?

4. What does Caroline say is required in order for you to become "a walking-on-water miracle to another person"? What else might happen as a result?

5. Caroline offers a list of "life-changing ideas." Which ones jump out at you? What other ideas might you add?

Chapter 2: What's Your Trigger?

1. Describe the event that turned out to be Caroline's "trigger." Why did this specific situation resonate with her? What was the immediate effect of her willingness to act? What happened long-term as a result of it?

2. What injustice grips your heart the most? If you don't already know your own trigger, what's one step you might take to figure it out?

3. Caroline says it's been her experience that when she gives her time to God, she gets more done in her personal life. How does this compare to your own experience? If you're not intentionally giving your time to God right now, are you willing to try it this week and see what happens?

4. Drawing from what you've learned in this chapter, what would you say to someone who is in the beginning stages of acting on her trigger—investing her time and energy in taking action—but isn't yet sure if it will succeed or how it's all going to play out?

Chapter 3: Serving and the Realities of Life

1. What are some of the keys to maintaining balance in your life? Why is this important to keep in mind as you're learning to "walk on water"?

2. What were the qualities Caroline admired most in Matthew when she was getting to know him? What qualities do you look for in your own relationships, and why are they important to you? What does that tell you about your own values? Can you identify ways in which they relate to your trigger and your purpose?

3. Think of a time when you found a special joy in serving. What made it a joyful experience for you?

Chapter 4: Look Long Enough

1. It can be tough and overwhelming to hear about others suffering, making us feel helpless. What does Caroline say is the solution? Why does she encourage us to look extra hard at those areas of injustice that we previously may have avoided? What would one of those be for you?

2. What is the difference between meeting a surface need and addressing a root problem? Would you say that one is ever more important than the other? Why or why not?

Chapter 5: Walk with Confidence

1. Caroline says, "The moment we take our eyes off Him is the moment we will start to feel the waves lapping around our ankles." Have you found it to be difficult to trust in Christ instead of your own abilities? What distractions do you face in your own faith walk? What helps you to keep your eyes on God?

2. Think about how discouraged Elijah was in 1 Kings 19. Now read the story of Elijah's courage in confronting King Ahab about his sin in 1 Kings 21:17-29 and note the king's response. What blessings would Elijah have missed had he given up? How can this encourage you next time you're feeling discouraged?

3. Caroline shares her experience that if you begin ministry with a willing heart, God will show up and provide financial resources. Yet many ministries do suffer financially; do you think this proves or disproves Caroline's

point? What can financial difficulties teach us about walking on water?

4. Do you feel confident in your calling? Take some time to pray that God will give you the courage to step out in willingness and the faith to believe He will not let you sink.

Chapter 6: The Fear of Being Unworthy

1. The first question the Dream Center asks women entering the program is, "What is your dream?" How would you answer this question?

2. Have you ever struggled with feeling unworthy to pursue your dream, to serve God, or to try to help others?

3. How does Caroline compare sin to drowning in this chapter? How do we get caught up in this? What practical things can we do to break the cycle of sin, insecurity, and self-doubt, and why do they help?

4. Caroline says that God can use you no matter who or where you are. Describe someone whom God used in unlikely circumstances and what happened as a result.

Chapter 7: Not Willing to Sink

1. When stepping out in faith, why is it so important to predetermine that sinking is simply not an option? How do you think we can tell the difference between giving up on something God has called us to do, and feeling the nudge from God telling us that we are not on the right path?

2. What is one specific way you can commit to starting tomorrow morning with hope and ending it with peace? How will this help you to stay afloat?

Chapter 8: Your Motivating Factor

1. How does God's love influence your decisions, your actions, and your attitude toward others?

2. What are some reasons people struggle to accept God's love? Take a moment to pray for anyone who doesn't feel loved by God—that He will communicate it to this person in a way he or she is willing to understand. How might you personally be a practical reflection of God's love to him or her?

3. Does knowing that "even at your best, you are not worthy" depress you or liberate you in your attitude toward serving others in God's name? How?

4. This chapter contains powerful stories about people experiencing God's love during difficult times. If you were contributing a story to this chapter, what person or situation would it be about?

Chapter 9: Our Wants vs. God's Wants

1. Why is it that your plans for your life and God's plans for your life may match up more than you think?

2. What is the difference between doing something out of fear of God and doing it out of a willing heart?

3. What role does the Holy Spirit have in our taking action to serve God?

Chapter 10: The *You* in Serving

1. What's the difference between having a wise reason not to do something and making an excuse to avoid it? How can our excuses hold us back from living God's promises?

2. There are 358 references in the Bible to helping the poor, the needy, the widow, and the orphan. Why do you think this issue is so important to God that He refers to it in His Word so many times? What are the benefits of paying attention to these needs? What are the risks if we ignore them?

3. How did Caroline find that serving others with a willing heart turned her complaints into praise? Think of one of your own complaints about your life (don't worry, we all have them!). How might you turn it around so that it becomes an opportunity for praise, thankfulness, and service?

Chapter 11: The Good Kind of Fear

1. What are some specific fears you have about taking action on your own trigger? Is it time? Money? Ability? Safety? What have you learned from this chapter about how to combat these fears?

2. What kind of fears would you say are appropriate and right to feel? How do you distinguish between those and the kind that hold you back from living out your purpose?

3. How does the knowledge that you are being obedient help to alleviate the stress of following your calling?

4. What were the keys to Caroline being able to face her fears and perform onstage for Matthew's anniversary present? Consider a fear that you're currently facing. Which of these keys speaks most to your heart? What might you do to act on it now?

Chapter 12: The Power of One

1. What examples from the Bible show us that one person matters to God? What does this mean to you? What does it mean when you think about making an impact through service?

2. When Caroline told God she was willing to live His dream for her life, she hoped that God would call her to serve somewhere exotic and far away. Yet her entire ministry has been based in LA. What might this teach us about God's call on our lives? How might it encourage us in moments when we don't seem to be getting what we want?

3. What did Peter have that gave him the ability to walk on water? What does this teach us about our own relationship with Christ?

4. Who is someone whom you've seen "walk on water" in your own life? How have his or her actions impacted you?

5. What does Caroline say is the key to being a good and faithful servant of God? What's something specific you can do this week to "get out of the boat" and put this principle into practice?

Notes

1. Todd M. Johnson and Kenneth R. Ross, eds., *Atlas of Global Christianity: 1910–2010* (Edinburgh: Edinburgh University Press, 2009), 69.
2. "Global Hunger Declining, But Still Unacceptably High," Food and Agriculture Organization of the United Nations, Economic and Social Development Department, September 2010, http://www.fao.org/docrep/012/al390e/al390e00.pdf.
3. "Global Hunger," Bread for the World, http://www.bread.org/hunger/global.
4. "Invisible: Slavery Today," National Underground Railroad Freedom Center, http://www.freedomcenter.org/slavery-today.
5. "Orphans in the World," NumberOf.net, last verified February 14, 2010, http://www.numberof.net/orphans-in-the-world.
6. Mother Teresa, *The Joy in Loving: A Guide to Daily Living*, comps. Jaya Chalika and Edward Le Joly (New York: Penguin, 2000), 146.
7. On April 21, 1993, Peter Digre, then director of the Los Angeles County Department of Children and Family Services, testified in a congressional hearing before the Subcommittee on Human Resources of the Committee on Ways and Means that about half of the removals of children from their homes are due to poverty and not abuse. "'It gets down to those very specific issues about a place to live, food on the table, medical care, and things like that,' he explained, adding that 'about half of the families are not physical abusers, not sexual abusers, not people with propensities to violence, but simply people who are struggling to keep ends pulled together and are eminently salvageable.'" Peter Digre's statements are documented in the book *President Clinton's Budget Proposal for New Funding for Child Welfare Services Targeted for Family Support and Preservation Services: Hearing before the Subcommittee on Human Resources of the Committee on Ways and Means, House of Representatives, One Hundred Third Congress, First Session, April 21, 1993* (Washington, DC: US Government Printing Office, 1993), 87–88. These statements are also

cited in "Los Angeles: The State Threatens a Takeover," The Institute for Psychological Therapies, http://www.ipt-forensics.com/journal/volume10 /j10_10_2.htm.

8. Troy Anderson,"Foster-Kid Cash Lure May Fade," *Los Angeles Daily News*, February 16, 2004, http://familyrights.us/news/archive/troy_anderson /fosterkid_cash_lure_may_fade.htm.

9. This statistic appears in President Barack Obama's press release on "National Foster Care Month," posted at Administration for Children & Families, US Department of Health and Human Services, April 29, 2011, http://www.acf .hhs.gov/national-foster-care-month.

10. Cited by the Lynchburg Literacy Council, http://lynchburgliteracy.org/?page _id=14.

11. Ibid.

12. "Illiteracy: A National Crisis, United Way's Role: A Report" (United Way of America, 1987), 9.

13. Cited by the Literacy Project Foundation, http://literacyprojectfoundation .org/community/statistics, and in Cynthia Brian's *Be the Star You Are! For Teens* (Garden City, NY: Morgan James Publishing, 2010), 256.

14. "My So-Called Emancipation: From Foster Care to Homelessness for California Youth," Human Rights Watch, May 20, 2010, page 1, http://www .cafosteringconnections.org/pdfs/My%20So-Called%20Emancipation-%20 Human%20Rghts%20Watch.pdf.

15. Cited in "Foster Care by the Numbers," Casey Family Programs, http://www .casey.org/newsroom/MediaKit/pdf/FosterCareByTheNumbers.pdf.

16. Bryce Christensen, "Fostering Confusion: What the 'Foster-Care Crisis' Really Means," *The Family in America Online Edition*, The Howard Center for Family, Religion, and Society 15, no. 5 (May 2001), http://www.profam.org /pub/fia/fia_1505.htm.

17. "Developmental Issues for Young Children in Foster Care," American Academy of Pediatrics, Committee on Early Childhood, Adoption, and Dependent Care, *Pediatrics* 106, no. 5 (November 1, 2000), http:// pediatrics.aappublications.org/content/106/5/1145.full.html (accessed November 21, 2012), 1146, 1148. See also "Multiple Placements in Foster Care: Literature Review of Correlates and Predictors," Children and Family Research Center, School of Social Work, University of Illinois at Urbana-Champaign, February 2004, http://cfrc.illinois.edu/pubs/lr_20040201 _MultiplePlacementsInFosterCare.pdf (accessed November 21, 2012).

18. Human Rights Watch interview with Phillip O., Whittier, age 22, April 24, 2006, quoted in "My So-Called Emancipation: From Foster Care to Homelessness for California Youth," Human Rights Watch, May 20, 2010, page 46, http://www.cafosteringconnections.org/pdfs/My%20So-Called%20 Emancipation-%20Human%20Rghts%20Watch.pdf.

19. "Foster Youth Education Initiative Releases Report on Improving Opportunities for Foster Youth," National Center for Youth Law, http://www .youthlaw.org/child_welfare/foster_youth_education_initiative.

20. "United Friends of the Children: Long-Term Commitments Leading to Lasting Impacts," *Giving Local*, January 28, 2011, http://give2network .wordpress.com/category/charities/child-welfare/united-friends-of-the-children. See also http://www.unitedfriends.org/about-ufc/faq.

21. "Co-Founders Wanted: MyFoco Provides Portal for Foster Youths (video)," posted February 21, 2011, http://www.centernetworks.com /myfoco-foster-youth-portal.

22. Mary Fairchild, "Christianity Today: General Statistics and Facts of Christianity," About.com, http://christianity.about.com/od/denominations /p/christiantoday.htm.

23. According to http://www.adoptuskids.org/meet-the-children, accessed November 21, 2012.

24. From an e-mail that the Dream Center received from DCFS on December 8, 2010.

25. Per http://www.safe-families.org/whatis_history.aspx.

26. Steven Ertelt, "New Planned Parenthood Report: Record Abortions Done in 2009," LifeNews.com, posted February 23, 2011, http://www.lifenews .com/2011/02/23/new-planned-parenthood-report-record-abortions-done-in-2009.

27. Michael Murray and James Wang, "Person of the Week: TOMS Shoes Founder Blake Mycoskie," ABC News, April 8, 2011, http://abcnews.go.com /International/PersonOfWeek/person-week-toms-shoes-founder-blake-mycoskie/story?id=13331473.

28. "Charity: Water," *Focusing Philanthropy*, http://www.focusingphilanthropy .org/registryitem.asp?ID=784&title=charity:%20water.

29. See http://www.watoto.com/about-us/the-founders/marilyn-skinner.

30. "Teaching Beyond Words," *Charisma Magazine*, http://www.charismamag .com/spirit/devotionals/live-extraordinarily?view=article&id=15026:teaching -beyond-words&catid=1505.

31. "Our History," *Convoy of Hope*, http://www.convoyofhope.org/go/who /our_history.

32. "The Changing Nature of Teen Addiction and Self-Harming," *Presentation Solutions*, May 10, 2011, http://presentationsolutions.org/2011/05/10 /nancy-alcorn/.

33. "Our Solution," *The A21 Campaign: Abolishing Injustice in the 21st Century*, http://www.thea21campaign.org/our-solution.php.

34. For more information, see Matthew Barnett, *The Cause within You* (Carol Stream, IL: Tyndale House Publishers, 2011), http://thecausewithinyou.com.

About the Authors

Caroline Barnett has a passion for inspiring women of the church to find their God-given cause. In her role at the Dream Center, Caroline has changed people's lives through a wide range of outreach ministries—from starting a food truck ministry that currently feeds over 50,000 people each month, to founding Project Prevention, a foster care intervention program designed to assist families facing the threat of separation due to issues of poverty. Caroline is married to Dream Center founder and *New York Times* bestselling author Matthew Barnett; they live with their two children in Los Angeles.

A. J. Gregory is an accomplished writer who has collaborated with fascinating high-profile figures on twenty-five books. She is also the author of *Silent Savior* and *Messy Faith*.

Online Discussion *guide*

TAKE *your* TYNDALE READING EXPERIENCE *to the* NEXT LEVEL

A FREE discussion guide for this book is available at bookclubhub.net, perfect for sparking conversations in your book group or for digging deeper into the text on your own.

www.bookclubhub.net

You'll also find free discussion guides for other Tyndale books, e-newsletters, e-mail devotionals, virtual book tours, and more!

DREAMCENTER

the church that never sleeps

The Dream Center, a volunteer driven organization that finds and fills the needs of individuals and families alike, was founded in 1994 and currently serves over 50,000 people each month.

2301 Bellevue Avenue | Los Angeles CA 90026 | 213.273.7000

DREAMCENTER.ORG

CP0655